ATS-4   ADMISSION TEST SERIES

This is your
PASSBOOK for...

Real Estate Salesman (RES)

Test Preparation Study Guide
Questions & Answers

COPYRIGHT NOTICE

This book is SOLELY intended for, is sold ONLY to, and its use is RESTRICTED to individual, bona fide applicants or candidates who qualify by virtue of having seriously filed applications for appropriate license, certificate, professional and/or promotional advancement, higher school matriculation, scholarship, or other legitimate requirements of education and/or governmental authorities.

This book is NOT intended for use, class instruction, tutoring, training, duplication, copying, reprinting, excerption, or adaptation, etc., by:

1) Other publishers
2) Proprietors and/or Instructors of "Coaching" and/or Preparatory Courses
3) Personnel and/or Training Divisions of commercial, industrial, and governmental organizations
4) Schools, colleges, or universities and/or their departments and staffs, including teachers and other personnel
5) Testing Agencies or Bureaus
6) Study groups which seek by the purchase of a single volume to copy and/or duplicate and/or adapt this material for use by the group as a whole without having purchased individual volumes for each of the members of the group
7) Et al.

Such persons would be in violation of appropriate Federal and State statutes.

PROVISION OF LICENSING AGREEMENTS – Recognized educational, commercial, industrial, and governmental institutions and organizations, and others legitimately engaged in educational pursuits, including training, testing, and measurement activities, may address request for a licensing agreement to the copyright owners, who will determine whether, and under what conditions, including fees and charges, the materials in this book may be used them. In other words, a licensing facility exists for the legitimate use of the material in this book on other than an individual basis. However, it is asseverated and affirmed here that the material in this book CANNOT be used without the receipt of the express permission of such a licensing agreement from the Publishers. Inquiries re licensing should be addressed to the company, attention rights and permissions department.

All rights reserved, including the right of reproduction in whole or in part, in any form or by any means, electronic or mechanical, including photocopying, recording, or by any information storage and retrieval system, without permission in writing from the Publisher.

Copyright © 2025 by
National Learning Corporation

212 Michael Drive, Syosset, NY 11791
(516) 921-8888 • www.passbooks.com
E-mail: info@passbooks.com

PASSBOOK® SERIES

THE *PASSBOOK® SERIES* has been created to prepare applicants and candidates for the ultimate academic battlefield – the examination room.

At some time in our lives, each and every one of us may be required to take an examination – for validation, matriculation, admission, qualification, registration, certification, or licensure.

Based on the assumption that every applicant or candidate has met the basic formal educational standards, has taken the required number of courses, and read the necessary texts, the *PASSBOOK® SERIES* furnishes the one special preparation which may assure passing with confidence, instead of failing with insecurity. Examination questions – together with answers – are furnished as the basic vehicle for study so that the mysteries of the examination and its compounding difficulties may be eliminated or diminished by a sure method.

This book is meant to help you pass your examination provided that you qualify and are serious in your objective.

The entire field is reviewed through the huge store of content information which is succinctly presented through a provocative and challenging approach – the question-and-answer method.

A climate of success is established by furnishing the correct answers at the end of each test.

You soon learn to recognize types of questions, forms of questions, and patterns of questioning. You may even begin to anticipate expected outcomes.

You perceive that many questions are repeated or adapted so that you can gain acute insights, which may enable you to score many sure points.

You learn how to confront new questions, or types of questions, and to attack them confidently and work out the correct answers.

You note objectives and emphases, and recognize pitfalls and dangers, so that you may make positive educational adjustments.

Moreover, you are kept fully informed in relation to new concepts, methods, practices, and directions in the field.

You discover that you are actually taking the examination all the time: you are preparing for the examination by "taking" an examination, not by reading extraneous and/or supererogatory textbooks.

In short, this PASSBOOK®, used directedly, should be an important factor in helping you to pass your test.

REAL ESTATE SALESMAN

DUTIES

A Real Estate Salesman (Salesperson) is a professional licensed to sell and procure sales of real property as well as procures rentals and leases of real property and is entitled to a fee for his or her services.

SCOPE OF THE EXAMINATION

The written test will be designed to test for knowledge, skills, and/or abilities in such areas as:
1. Real property terminology, documents and forms;
2. Real property law; and
3. Real estate license law and practice.

HOW TO TAKE A TEST

I. YOU MUST PASS AN EXAMINATION

A. *WHAT EVERY CANDIDATE SHOULD KNOW*

Examination applicants often ask us for help in preparing for the written test. What can I study in advance? What kinds of questions will be asked? How will the test be given? How will the papers be graded?

As an applicant for a civil service examination, you may be wondering about some of these things. Our purpose here is to suggest effective methods of advance study and to describe civil service examinations.

Your chances for success on this examination can be increased if you know how to prepare. Those "pre-examination jitters" can be reduced if you know what to expect. You can even experience an adventure in good citizenship if you know why civil service exams are given.

B. *WHY ARE CIVIL SERVICE EXAMINATIONS GIVEN?*

Civil service examinations are important to you in two ways. As a citizen, you want public jobs filled by employees who know how to do their work. As a job seeker, you want a fair chance to compete for that job on an equal footing with other candidates. The best-known means of accomplishing this two-fold goal is the competitive examination.

Exams are widely publicized throughout the nation. They may be administered for jobs in federal, state, city, municipal, town or village governments or agencies.

Any citizen may apply, with some limitations, such as the age or residence of applicants. Your experience and education may be reviewed to see whether you meet the requirements for the particular examination. When these requirements exist, they are reasonable and applied consistently to all applicants. Thus, a competitive examination may cause you some uneasiness now, but it is your privilege and safeguard.

C. *HOW ARE CIVIL SERVICE EXAMS DEVELOPED?*

Examinations are carefully written by trained technicians who are specialists in the field known as "psychological measurement," in consultation with recognized authorities in the field of work that the test will cover. These experts recommend the subject matter areas or skills to be tested; only those knowledges or skills important to your success on the job are included. The most reliable books and source materials available are used as references. Together, the experts and technicians judge the difficulty level of the questions.

Test technicians know how to phrase questions so that the problem is clearly stated. Their ethics do not permit "trick" or "catch" questions. Questions may have been tried out on sample groups, or subjected to statistical analysis, to determine their usefulness.

Written tests are often used in combination with performance tests, ratings of training and experience, and oral interviews. All of these measures combine to form the best-known means of finding the right person for the right job.

II. HOW TO PASS THE WRITTEN TEST

A. NATURE OF THE EXAMINATION

To prepare intelligently for civil service examinations, you should know how they differ from school examinations you have taken. In school you were assigned certain definite pages to read or subjects to cover. The examination questions were quite detailed and usually emphasized memory. Civil service exams, on the other hand, try to discover your present ability to perform the duties of a position, plus your potentiality to learn these duties. In other words, a civil service exam attempts to predict how successful you will be. Questions cover such a broad area that they cannot be as minute and detailed as school exam questions.

In the public service similar kinds of work, or positions, are grouped together in one "class." This process is known as *position-classification*. All the positions in a class are paid according to the salary range for that class. One class title covers all of these positions, and they are all tested by the same examination.

B. FOUR BASIC STEPS

1) Study the announcement

How, then, can you know what subjects to study? Our best answer is: "Learn as much as possible about the class of positions for which you've applied." The exam will test the knowledge, skills and abilities needed to do the work.

Your most valuable source of information about the position you want is the official exam announcement. This announcement lists the training and experience qualifications. Check these standards and apply only if you come reasonably close to meeting them.

The brief description of the position in the examination announcement offers some clues to the subjects which will be tested. Think about the job itself. Review the duties in your mind. Can you perform them, or are there some in which you are rusty? Fill in the blank spots in your preparation.

Many jurisdictions preview the written test in the exam announcement by including a section called "Knowledge and Abilities Required," "Scope of the Examination," or some similar heading. Here you will find out specifically what fields will be tested.

2) Review your own background

Once you learn in general what the position is all about, and what you need to know to do the work, ask yourself which subjects you already know fairly well and which need improvement. You may wonder whether to concentrate on improving your strong areas or on building some background in your fields of weakness. When the announcement has specified "some knowledge" or "considerable knowledge," or has used adjectives like "beginning principles of..." or "advanced ... methods," you can get a clue as to the number and difficulty of questions to be asked in any given field. More questions, and hence broader coverage, would be included for those subjects which are more important in the work. Now weigh your strengths and weaknesses against the job requirements and prepare accordingly.

3) Determine the level of the position

Another way to tell how intensively you should prepare is to understand the level of the job for which you are applying. Is it the entering level? In other words, is this the position in which beginners in a field of work are hired? Or is it an intermediate or advanced level? Sometimes this is indicated by such words as "Junior" or "Senior" in the class title. Other jurisdictions use Roman numerals to designate the level – Clerk I, Clerk II, for example. The word "Supervisor" sometimes appears in the title. If the level is not indicated by the title, check the description of duties. Will you be working under very close supervision, or will you have responsibility for independent decisions in this work?

4) Choose appropriate study materials

Now that you know the subjects to be examined and the relative amount of each subject to be covered, you can choose suitable study materials. For beginning level jobs, or even advanced ones, if you have a pronounced weakness in some aspect of your training, read a modern, standard textbook in that field. Be sure it is up to date and has general coverage. Such books are normally available at your library, and the librarian will be glad to help you locate one. For entry-level positions, questions of appropriate difficulty are chosen – neither highly advanced questions, nor those too simple. Such questions require careful thought but not advanced training.

If the position for which you are applying is technical or advanced, you will read more advanced, specialized material. If you are already familiar with the basic principles of your field, elementary textbooks would waste your time. Concentrate on advanced textbooks and technical periodicals. Think through the concepts and review difficult problems in your field.

These are all general sources. You can get more ideas on your own initiative, following these leads. For example, training manuals and publications of the government agency which employs workers in your field can be useful, particularly for technical and professional positions. A letter or visit to the government department involved may result in more specific study suggestions, and certainly will provide you with a more definite idea of the exact nature of the position you are seeking.

III. KINDS OF TESTS

Tests are used for purposes other than measuring knowledge and ability to perform specified duties. For some positions, it is equally important to test ability to make adjustments to new situations or to profit from training. In others, basic mental abilities not dependent on information are essential. Questions which test these things may not appear as pertinent to the duties of the position as those which test for knowledge and information. Yet they are often highly important parts of a fair examination. For very general questions, it is almost impossible to help you direct your study efforts. What we can do is to point out some of the more common of these general abilities needed in public service positions and describe some typical questions.

1) General information

Broad, general information has been found useful for predicting job success in some kinds of work. This is tested in a variety of ways, from vocabulary lists to questions about current events. Basic background in some field of work, such as sociology or economics, may be sampled in a group of questions. Often these are principles which have become familiar to most persons through exposure rather than through formal training. It is difficult to advise you how to study for these questions; being alert to the world around you is our best suggestion.

2) Verbal ability

An example of an ability needed in many positions is verbal or language ability. Verbal ability is, in brief, the ability to use and understand words. Vocabulary and grammar tests are typical measures of this ability. Reading comprehension or paragraph interpretation questions are common in many kinds of civil service tests. You are given a paragraph of written material and asked to find its central meaning.

3) Numerical ability

Number skills can be tested by the familiar arithmetic problem, by checking paired lists of numbers to see which are alike and which are different, or by interpreting charts and graphs. In the latter test, a graph may be printed in the test booklet which you are asked to use as the basis for answering questions.

4) Observation

A popular test for law-enforcement positions is the observation test. A picture is shown to you for several minutes, then taken away. Questions about the picture test your ability to observe both details and larger elements.

5) Following directions

In many positions in the public service, the employee must be able to carry out written instructions dependably and accurately. You may be given a chart with several columns, each column listing a variety of information. The questions require you to carry out directions involving the information given in the chart.

6) Skills and aptitudes

Performance tests effectively measure some manual skills and aptitudes. When the skill is one in which you are trained, such as typing or shorthand, you can practice. These tests are often very much like those given in business school or high school courses. For many of the other skills and aptitudes, however, no short-time preparation can be made. Skills and abilities natural to you or that you have developed throughout your lifetime are being tested.

Many of the general questions just described provide all the data needed to answer the questions and ask you to use your reasoning ability to find the answers. Your best preparation for these tests, as well as for tests of facts and ideas, is to be at your physical and mental best. You, no doubt, have your own methods of getting into an exam-taking mood and keeping "in shape." The next section lists some ideas on this subject.

IV. KINDS OF QUESTIONS

Only rarely is the "essay" question, which you answer in narrative form, used in civil service tests. Civil service tests are usually of the short-answer type. Full instructions for answering these questions will be given to you at the examination. But in case this is your first experience with short-answer questions and separate answer sheets, here is what you need to know:

1) Multiple-choice Questions

Most popular of the short-answer questions is the "multiple choice" or "best answer" question. It can be used, for example, to test for factual knowledge, ability to solve problems or judgment in meeting situations found at work.

A multiple-choice question is normally one of three types—
- It can begin with an incomplete statement followed by several possible endings. You are to find the one ending which *best* completes the statement, although some of the others may not be entirely wrong.
- It can also be a complete statement in the form of a question which is answered by choosing one of the statements listed.

- It can be in the form of a problem – again you select the best answer.

Here is an example of a multiple-choice question with a discussion which should give you some clues as to the method for choosing the right answer:

When an employee has a complaint about his assignment, the action which will *best* help him overcome his difficulty is to
- A. discuss his difficulty with his coworkers
- B. take the problem to the head of the organization
- C. take the problem to the person who gave him the assignment
- D. say nothing to anyone about his complaint

In answering this question, you should study each of the choices to find which is best. Consider choice "A" – Certainly an employee may discuss his complaint with fellow employees, but no change or improvement can result, and the complaint remains unresolved. Choice "B" is a poor choice since the head of the organization probably does not know what assignment you have been given, and taking your problem to him is known as "going over the head" of the supervisor. The supervisor, or person who made the assignment, is the person who can clarify it or correct any injustice. Choice "C" is, therefore, correct. To say nothing, as in choice "D," is unwise. Supervisors have and interest in knowing the problems employees are facing, and the employee is seeking a solution to his problem.

2) True/False Questions

The "true/false" or "right/wrong" form of question is sometimes used. Here a complete statement is given. Your job is to decide whether the statement is right or wrong.

SAMPLE: A roaming cell-phone call to a nearby city costs less than a non-roaming call to a distant city.

This statement is wrong, or false, since roaming calls are more expensive.

This is not a complete list of all possible question forms, although most of the others are variations of these common types. You will always get complete directions for answering questions. Be sure you understand *how* to mark your answers – ask questions until you do.

V. RECORDING YOUR ANSWERS

Computer terminals are used more and more today for many different kinds of exams.

For an examination with very few applicants, you may be told to record your answers in the test booklet itself. Separate answer sheets are much more common. If this separate answer sheet is to be scored by machine – and this is often the case – it is highly important that you mark your answers correctly in order to get credit.

An electronic scoring machine is often used in civil service offices because of the speed with which papers can be scored. Machine-scored answer sheets must be marked with a pencil, which will be given to you. This pencil has a high graphite content which responds to the electronic scoring machine. As a matter of fact, stray dots may register as answers, so do not let your pencil rest on the answer sheet while you are pondering the correct answer. Also, if your pencil lead breaks or is otherwise defective, ask for another.

Since the answer sheet will be dropped in a slot in the scoring machine, be careful not to bend the corners or get the paper crumpled.

The answer sheet normally has five vertical columns of numbers, with 30 numbers to a column. These numbers correspond to the question numbers in your test booklet. After each number, going across the page are four or five pairs of dotted lines. These short dotted lines have small letters or numbers above them. The first two pairs may also have a "T" or "F" above the letters. This indicates that the first two pairs only are to be used if the questions are of the true-false type. If the questions are multiple choice, disregard the "T" and "F" and pay attention only to the small letters or numbers.

Answer your questions in the manner of the sample that follows:

32. The largest city in the United States is
    A. Washington, D.C.
    B. New York City
    C. Chicago
    D. Detroit
    E. San Francisco

1) Choose the answer you think is best. (New York City is the largest, so "B" is correct.)
2) Find the row of dotted lines numbered the same as the question you are answering. (Find row number 32)
3) Find the pair of dotted lines corresponding to the answer. (Find the pair of lines under the mark "B.")
4) Make a solid black mark between the dotted lines.

VI. BEFORE THE TEST

Common sense will help you find procedures to follow to get ready for an examination. Too many of us, however, overlook these sensible measures. Indeed, nervousness and fatigue have been found to be the most serious reasons why applicants fail to do their best on civil service tests. Here is a list of reminders:

- Begin your preparation early – Don't wait until the last minute to go scurrying around for books and materials or to find out what the position is all about.
- Prepare continuously – An hour a night for a week is better than an all-night cram session. This has been definitely established. What is more, a night a week for a month will return better dividends than crowding your study into a shorter period of time.
- Locate the place of the exam – You have been sent a notice telling you when and where to report for the examination. If the location is in a different town or otherwise unfamiliar to you, it would be well to inquire the best route and learn something about the building.
- Relax the night before the test – Allow your mind to rest. Do not study at all that night. Plan some mild recreation or diversion; then go to bed early and get a good night's sleep.
- Get up early enough to make a leisurely trip to the place for the test – This way unforeseen events, traffic snarls, unfamiliar buildings, etc. will not upset you.
- Dress comfortably – A written test is not a fashion show. You will be known by number and not by name, so wear something comfortable.

- Leave excess paraphernalia at home – Shopping bags and odd bundles will get in your way. You need bring only the items mentioned in the official notice you received; usually everything you need is provided. Do not bring reference books to the exam. They will only confuse those last minutes and be taken away from you when in the test room.
- Arrive somewhat ahead of time – If because of transportation schedules you must get there very early, bring a newspaper or magazine to take your mind off yourself while waiting.
- Locate the examination room – When you have found the proper room, you will be directed to the seat or part of the room where you will sit. Sometimes you are given a sheet of instructions to read while you are waiting. Do not fill out any forms until you are told to do so; just read them and be prepared.
- Relax and prepare to listen to the instructions
- If you have any physical problem that may keep you from doing your best, be sure to tell the test administrator. If you are sick or in poor health, you really cannot do your best on the exam. You can come back and take the test some other time.

VII. AT THE TEST

The day of the test is here and you have the test booklet in your hand. The temptation to get going is very strong. Caution! There is more to success than knowing the right answers. You must know how to identify your papers and understand variations in the type of short-answer question used in this particular examination. Follow these suggestions for maximum results from your efforts:

1) Cooperate with the monitor

The test administrator has a duty to create a situation in which you can be as much at ease as possible. He will give instructions, tell you when to begin, check to see that you are marking your answer sheet correctly, and so on. He is not there to guard you, although he will see that your competitors do not take unfair advantage. He wants to help you do your best.

2) Listen to all instructions

Don't jump the gun! Wait until you understand all directions. In most civil service tests you get more time than you need to answer the questions. So don't be in a hurry. Read each word of instructions until you clearly understand the meaning. Study the examples, listen to all announcements and follow directions. Ask questions if you do not understand what to do.

3) Identify your papers

Civil service exams are usually identified by number only. You will be assigned a number; you must not put your name on your test papers. Be sure to copy your number correctly. Since more than one exam may be given, copy your exact examination title.

4) Plan your time

Unless you are told that a test is a "speed" or "rate of work" test, speed itself is usually not important. Time enough to answer all the questions will be provided, but this does not mean that you have all day. An overall time limit has been set. Divide the total time (in minutes) by the number of questions to determine the approximate time you have for each question.

5) Do not linger over difficult questions

If you come across a difficult question, mark it with a paper clip (useful to have along) and come back to it when you have been through the booklet. One caution if you do this – be sure to skip a number on your answer sheet as well. Check often to be sure that you have not lost your place and that you are marking in the row numbered the same as the question you are answering.

6) Read the questions

Be sure you know what the question asks! Many capable people are unsuccessful because they failed to *read* the questions correctly.

7) Answer all questions

Unless you have been instructed that a penalty will be deducted for incorrect answers, it is better to guess than to omit a question.

8) Speed tests

It is often better NOT to guess on speed tests. It has been found that on timed tests people are tempted to spend the last few seconds before time is called in marking answers at random – without even reading them – in the hope of picking up a few extra points. To discourage this practice, the instructions may warn you that your score will be "corrected" for guessing. That is, a penalty will be applied. The incorrect answers will be deducted from the correct ones, or some other penalty formula will be used.

9) Review your answers

If you finish before time is called, go back to the questions you guessed or omitted to give them further thought. Review other answers if you have time.

10) Return your test materials

If you are ready to leave before others have finished or time is called, take ALL your materials to the monitor and leave quietly. Never take any test material with you. The monitor can discover whose papers are not complete, and taking a test booklet may be grounds for disqualification.

VIII. EXAMINATION TECHNIQUES

1) Read the general instructions carefully. These are usually printed on the first page of the exam booklet. As a rule, these instructions refer to the timing of the examination; the fact that you should not start work until the signal and must stop work at a signal, etc. If there are any *special* instructions, such as a choice of questions to be answered, make sure that you note this instruction carefully.

2) When you are ready to start work on the examination, that is as soon as the signal has been given, read the instructions to each question booklet, underline any key words or phrases, such as *least, best, outline, describe* and the like. In this way you will tend to answer as requested rather than discover on reviewing your paper that you *listed without describing*, that you selected the *worst* choice rather than the *best* choice, etc.

3) If the examination is of the objective or multiple-choice type – that is, each question will also give a series of possible answers: A, B, C or D, and you are called upon to select the best answer and write the letter next to that answer on your answer paper – it is advisable to start answering each question in turn. There may be anywhere from 50 to 100 such questions in the three or four hours allotted and you can see how much time would be taken if you read through all the questions before beginning to answer any. Furthermore, if you come across a question or group of questions which you know would be difficult to answer, it would undoubtedly affect your handling of all the other questions.

4) If the examination is of the essay type and contains but a few questions, it is a moot point as to whether you should read all the questions before starting to answer any one. Of course, if you are given a choice – say five out of seven and the like – then it is essential to read all the questions so you can eliminate the two that are most difficult. If, however, you are asked to answer all the questions, there may be danger in trying to answer the easiest one first because you may find that you will spend too much time on it. The best technique is to answer the first question, then proceed to the second, etc.

5) Time your answers. Before the exam begins, write down the time it started, then add the time allowed for the examination and write down the time it must be completed, then divide the time available somewhat as follows:
   - If 3-1/2 hours are allowed, that would be 210 minutes. If you have 80 objective-type questions, that would be an average of 2-1/2 minutes per question. Allow yourself no more than 2 minutes per question, or a total of 160 minutes, which will permit about 50 minutes to review.
   - If for the time allotment of 210 minutes there are 7 essay questions to answer, that would average about 30 minutes a question. Give yourself only 25 minutes per question so that you have about 35 minutes to review.

6) The most important instruction is to *read each question* and make sure you know what is wanted. The second most important instruction is to *time yourself properly* so that you answer every question. The third most important instruction is to *answer every question*. Guess if you have to but include something for each question. Remember that you will receive no credit for a blank and will probably receive some credit if you write something in answer to an essay question. If you guess a letter – say "B" for a multiple-choice question – you may have guessed right. If you leave a blank as an answer to a multiple-choice question, the examiners may respect your feelings but it will not add a point to your score. Some exams may penalize you for wrong answers, so in such cases *only*, you may not want to guess unless you have some basis for your answer.

7) Suggestions
   a. Objective-type questions
      1. Examine the question booklet for proper sequence of pages and questions
      2. Read all instructions carefully
      3. Skip any question which seems too difficult; return to it after all other questions have been answered
      4. Apportion your time properly; do not spend too much time on any single question or group of questions

5. Note and underline key words – *all, most, fewest, least, best, worst, same, opposite*, etc.
6. Pay particular attention to negatives
7. Note unusual option, e.g., unduly long, short, complex, different or similar in content to the body of the question
8. Observe the use of "hedging" words – *probably, may, most likely*, etc.
9. Make sure that your answer is put next to the same number as the question
10. Do not second-guess unless you have good reason to believe the second answer is definitely more correct
11. Cross out original answer if you decide another answer is more accurate; do not erase until you are ready to hand your paper in
12. Answer all questions; guess unless instructed otherwise
13. Leave time for review

   b. Essay questions
   1. Read each question carefully
   2. Determine exactly what is wanted. Underline key words or phrases.
   3. Decide on outline or paragraph answer
   4. Include many different points and elements unless asked to develop any one or two points or elements
   5. Show impartiality by giving pros and cons unless directed to select one side only
   6. Make and write down any assumptions you find necessary to answer the questions
   7. Watch your English, grammar, punctuation and choice of words
   8. Time your answers; don't crowd material

8) Answering the essay question

Most essay questions can be answered by framing the specific response around several key words or ideas. Here are a few such key words or ideas:

M's: manpower, materials, methods, money, management
P's: purpose, program, policy, plan, procedure, practice, problems, pitfalls, personnel, public relations

   a. Six basic steps in handling problems:
   1. Preliminary plan and background development
   2. Collect information, data and facts
   3. Analyze and interpret information, data and facts
   4. Analyze and develop solutions as well as make recommendations
   5. Prepare report and sell recommendations
   6. Install recommendations and follow up effectiveness

   b. Pitfalls to avoid
   1. *Taking things for granted* – A statement of the situation does not necessarily imply that each of the elements is necessarily true; for example, a complaint may be invalid and biased so that all that can be taken for granted is that a complaint has been registered

2. *Considering only one side of a situation* – Wherever possible, indicate several alternatives and then point out the reasons you selected the best one
3. *Failing to indicate follow up* – Whenever your answer indicates action on your part, make certain that you will take proper follow-up action to see how successful your recommendations, procedures or actions turn out to be
4. *Taking too long in answering any single question* – Remember to time your answers properly

IX. AFTER THE TEST

Scoring procedures differ in detail among civil service jurisdictions although the general principles are the same. Whether the papers are hand-scored or graded by machine we have described, they are nearly always graded by number. That is, the person who marks the paper knows only the number – never the name – of the applicant. Not until all the papers have been graded will they be matched with names. If other tests, such as training and experience or oral interview ratings have been given, scores will be combined. Different parts of the examination usually have different weights. For example, the written test might count 60 percent of the final grade, and a rating of training and experience 40 percent. In many jurisdictions, veterans will have a certain number of points added to their grades.

After the final grade has been determined, the names are placed in grade order and an eligible list is established. There are various methods for resolving ties between those who get the same final grade – probably the most common is to place first the name of the person whose application was received first. Job offers are made from the eligible list in the order the names appear on it. You will be notified of your grade and your rank as soon as all these computations have been made. This will be done as rapidly as possible.

People who are found to meet the requirements in the announcement are called "eligibles." Their names are put on a list of eligible candidates. An eligible's chances of getting a job depend on how high he stands on this list and how fast agencies are filling jobs from the list.

When a job is to be filled from a list of eligibles, the agency asks for the names of people on the list of eligibles for that job. When the civil service commission receives this request, it sends to the agency the names of the three people highest on this list. Or, if the job to be filled has specialized requirements, the office sends the agency the names of the top three persons who meet these requirements from the general list.

The appointing officer makes a choice from among the three people whose names were sent to him. If the selected person accepts the appointment, the names of the others are put back on the list to be considered for future openings.

That is the rule in hiring from all kinds of eligible lists, whether they are for typist, carpenter, chemist, or something else. For every vacancy, the appointing officer has his choice of any one of the top three eligibles on the list. This explains why the person whose name is on top of the list sometimes does not get an appointment when some of the persons lower on the list do. If the appointing officer chooses the second or third eligible, the No. 1 eligible does not get a job at once, but stays on the list until he is appointed or the list is terminated.

X. HOW TO PASS THE INTERVIEW TEST

The examination for which you applied requires an oral interview test. You have already taken the written test and you are now being called for the interview test – the final part of the formal examination.

You may think that it is not possible to prepare for an interview test and that there are no procedures to follow during an interview. Our purpose is to point out some things you can do in advance that will help you and some good rules to follow and pitfalls to avoid while you are being interviewed.

What is an interview supposed to test?

The written examination is designed to test the technical knowledge and competence of the candidate; the oral is designed to evaluate intangible qualities, not readily measured otherwise, and to establish a list showing the relative fitness of each candidate – as measured against his competitors – for the position sought. Scoring is not on the basis of "right" and "wrong," but on a sliding scale of values ranging from "not passable" to "outstanding." As a matter of fact, it is possible to achieve a relatively low score without a single "incorrect" answer because of evident weakness in the qualities being measured.

Occasionally, an examination may consist entirely of an oral test – either an individual or a group oral. In such cases, information is sought concerning the technical knowledges and abilities of the candidate, since there has been no written examination for this purpose. More commonly, however, an oral test is used to supplement a written examination.

Who conducts interviews?

The composition of oral boards varies among different jurisdictions. In nearly all, a representative of the personnel department serves as chairman. One of the members of the board may be a representative of the department in which the candidate would work. In some cases, "outside experts" are used, and, frequently, a businessman or some other representative of the general public is asked to serve. Labor and management or other special groups may be represented. The aim is to secure the services of experts in the appropriate field.

However the board is composed, it is a good idea (and not at all improper or unethical) to ascertain in advance of the interview who the members are and what groups they represent. When you are introduced to them, you will have some idea of their backgrounds and interests, and at least you will not stutter and stammer over their names.

What should be done before the interview?

While knowledge about the board members is useful and takes some of the surprise element out of the interview, there is other preparation which is more substantive. It *is* possible to prepare for an oral interview – in several ways:

1) Keep a copy of your application and review it carefully before the interview

This may be the only document before the oral board, and the starting point of the interview. Know what education and experience you have listed there, and the sequence and dates of all of it. Sometimes the board will ask you to review the highlights of your experience for them; you should not have to hem and haw doing it.

2) Study the class specification and the examination announcement

Usually, the oral board has one or both of these to guide them. The qualities, characteristics or knowledges required by the position sought are stated in these documents. They offer valuable clues as to the nature of the oral interview. For example, if the job involves supervisory responsibilities, the announcement will usually indicate that knowledge of modern supervisory methods and the qualifications of the candidate as a supervisor will be tested. If so, you can expect such questions, frequently in the form of a hypothetical situation which you are expected to solve. NEVER go into an oral without knowledge of the duties and responsibilities of the job you seek.

3) Think through each qualification required

Try to visualize the kind of questions you would ask if you were a board member. How well could you answer them? Try especially to appraise your own knowledge and background in each area, *measured against the job sought*, and identify any areas in which you are weak. Be critical and realistic – do not flatter yourself.

4) Do some general reading in areas in which you feel you may be weak

For example, if the job involves supervision and your past experience has NOT, some general reading in supervisory methods and practices, particularly in the field of human relations, might be useful. Do NOT study agency procedures or detailed manuals. The oral board will be testing your understanding and capacity, not your memory.

5) Get a good night's sleep and watch your general health and mental attitude

You will want a clear head at the interview. Take care of a cold or any other minor ailment, and of course, no hangovers.

What should be done on the day of the interview?

Now comes the day of the interview itself. Give yourself plenty of time to get there. Plan to arrive somewhat ahead of the scheduled time, particularly if your appointment is in the fore part of the day. If a previous candidate fails to appear, the board might be ready for you a bit early. By early afternoon an oral board is almost invariably behind schedule if there are many candidates, and you may have to wait. Take along a book or magazine to read, or your application to review, but leave any extraneous material in the waiting room when you go in for your interview. In any event, relax and compose yourself.

The matter of dress is important. The board is forming impressions about you – from your experience, your manners, your attitude, and your appearance. Give your personal appearance careful attention. Dress your best, but not your flashiest. Choose conservative, appropriate clothing, and be sure it is immaculate. This is a business interview, and your appearance should indicate that you regard it as such. Besides, being well groomed and properly dressed will help boost your confidence.

Sooner or later, someone will call your name and escort you into the interview room. *This is it.* From here on you are on your own. It is too late for any more preparation. But remember, you asked for this opportunity to prove your fitness, and you are here because your request was granted.

What happens when you go in?

The usual sequence of events will be as follows: The clerk (who is often the board stenographer) will introduce you to the chairman of the oral board, who will introduce you to the other members of the board. Acknowledge the introductions before you sit down. Do not be surprised if you find a microphone facing you or a stenotypist sitting by. Oral interviews are usually recorded in the event of an appeal or other review.

Usually the chairman of the board will open the interview by reviewing the highlights of your education and work experience from your application – primarily for the benefit of the other members of the board, as well as to get the material into the record. Do not interrupt or comment unless there is an error or significant misinterpretation; if that is the case, do not hesitate. But do not quibble about insignificant matters. Also, he will usually ask you some question about your education, experience or your present job – partly to get you to start talking and to establish the interviewing "rapport." He may start the actual questioning, or turn it over to one of the other members. Frequently, each member undertakes the questioning on a particular area, one in which he is perhaps most competent, so you can expect each member to participate in the examination. Because time is limited, you may also expect some rather abrupt switches in the direction the questioning takes, so do not be upset by it. Normally, a board member will not pursue a single line of questioning unless he discovers a particular strength or weakness.

After each member has participated, the chairman will usually ask whether any member has any further questions, then will ask you if you have anything you wish to add. Unless you are expecting this question, it may floor you. Worse, it may start you off on an extended, extemporaneous speech. The board is not usually seeking more information. The question is principally to offer you a last opportunity to present further qualifications or to indicate that you have nothing to add. So, if you feel that a significant qualification or characteristic has been overlooked, it is proper to point it out in a sentence or so. Do not compliment the board on the thoroughness of their examination – they have been sketchy, and you know it. If you wish, merely say, "No thank you, I have nothing further to add." This is a point where you can "talk yourself out" of a good impression or fail to present an important bit of information. Remember, *you close the interview yourself*.

The chairman will then say, "That is all, Mr. _____, thank you." Do not be startled; the interview is over, and quicker than you think. Thank him, gather your belongings and take your leave. Save your sigh of relief for the other side of the door.

How to put your best foot forward

Throughout this entire process, you may feel that the board individually and collectively is trying to pierce your defenses, seek out your hidden weaknesses and embarrass and confuse you. Actually, this is not true. They are obliged to make an appraisal of your qualifications for the job you are seeking, and they want to see you in your best light. Remember, they must interview all candidates and a non-cooperative candidate may become a failure in spite of their best efforts to bring out his qualifications. Here are 15 suggestions that will help you:

1) Be natural – Keep your attitude confident, not cocky

If you are not confident that you can do the job, do not expect the board to be. Do not apologize for your weaknesses, try to bring out your strong points. The board is interested in a positive, not negative, presentation. Cockiness will antagonize any board member and make him wonder if you are covering up a weakness by a false show of strength.

2) Get comfortable, but don't lounge or sprawl

Sit erectly but not stiffly. A careless posture may lead the board to conclude that you are careless in other things, or at least that you are not impressed by the importance of the occasion. Either conclusion is natural, even if incorrect. Do not fuss with your clothing, a pencil or an ashtray. Your hands may occasionally be useful to emphasize a point; do not let them become a point of distraction.

3) Do not wisecrack or make small talk

This is a serious situation, and your attitude should show that you consider it as such. Further, the time of the board is limited – they do not want to waste it, and neither should you.

4) Do not exaggerate your experience or abilities

In the first place, from information in the application or other interviews and sources, the board may know more about you than you think. Secondly, you probably will not get away with it. An experienced board is rather adept at spotting such a situation, so do not take the chance.

5) If you know a board member, do not make a point of it, yet do not hide it

Certainly you are not fooling him, and probably not the other members of the board. Do not try to take advantage of your acquaintanceship – it will probably do you little good.

6) Do not dominate the interview

Let the board do that. They will give you the clues – do not assume that you have to do all the talking. Realize that the board has a number of questions to ask you, and do not try to take up all the interview time by showing off your extensive knowledge of the answer to the first one.

7) Be attentive

You only have 20 minutes or so, and you should keep your attention at its sharpest throughout. When a member is addressing a problem or question to you, give him your undivided attention. Address your reply principally to him, but do not exclude the other board members.

8) Do not interrupt

A board member may be stating a problem for you to analyze. He will ask you a question when the time comes. Let him state the problem, and wait for the question.

9) Make sure you understand the question

Do not try to answer until you are sure what the question is. If it is not clear, restate it in your own words or ask the board member to clarify it for you. However, do not haggle about minor elements.

10) Reply promptly but not hastily

A common entry on oral board rating sheets is "candidate responded readily," or "candidate hesitated in replies." Respond as promptly and quickly as you can, but do not jump to a hasty, ill-considered answer.

11) Do not be peremptory in your answers

A brief answer is proper – but do not fire your answer back. That is a losing game from your point of view. The board member can probably ask questions much faster than you can answer them.

12) Do not try to create the answer you think the board member wants

He is interested in what kind of mind you have and how it works – not in playing games. Furthermore, he can usually spot this practice and will actually grade you down on it.

13) Do not switch sides in your reply merely to agree with a board member

Frequently, a member will take a contrary position merely to draw you out and to see if you are willing and able to defend your point of view. Do not start a debate, yet do not surrender a good position. If a position is worth taking, it is worth defending.

14) Do not be afraid to admit an error in judgment if you are shown to be wrong

The board knows that you are forced to reply without any opportunity for careful consideration. Your answer may be demonstrably wrong. If so, admit it and get on with the interview.

15) Do not dwell at length on your present job

The opening question may relate to your present assignment. Answer the question but do not go into an extended discussion. You are being examined for a *new* job, not your present one. As a matter of fact, try to phrase ALL your answers in terms of the job for which you are being examined.

Basis of Rating

Probably you will forget most of these "do's" and "don'ts" when you walk into the oral interview room. Even remembering them all will not ensure you a passing grade. Perhaps you did not have the qualifications in the first place. But remembering them will help you to put your best foot forward, without treading on the toes of the board members.

Rumor and popular opinion to the contrary notwithstanding, an oral board wants you to make the best appearance possible. They know you are under pressure – but they also want to see how you respond to it as a guide to what your reaction would be under the pressures of the job you seek. They will be influenced by the degree of poise you display, the personal traits you show and the manner in which you respond.

ABOUT THIS BOOK

This book contains tests divided into Examination Sections. Go through each test, answering every question in the margin. We have also attached a sample answer sheet at the back of the book that can be removed and used. At the end of each test look at the answer key and check your answers. On the ones you got wrong, look at the right answer choice and learn. Do not fill in the answers first. Do not memorize the questions and answers, but understand the answer and principles involved. On your test, the questions will likely be different from the samples. Questions are changed and new ones added. If you understand these past questions you should have success with any changes that arise. Tests may consist of several types of questions. We have additional books on each subject should more study be advisable or necessary for you. Finally, the more you study, the better prepared you will be. This book is intended to be the last thing you study before you walk into the examination room. Prior study of relevant texts is also recommended. NLC publishes some of these in our Fundamental Series. Knowledge and good sense are important factors in passing your exam. Good luck also helps. So now study this Passbook, absorb the material contained within and take that knowledge into the examination. Then do your best to pass that exam.

EXAMINATION SECTION

EXAMINATION SECTION
TEST 1

DIRECTIONS: Each question or incomplete statement is followed by several suggested answers or completions. Select the one that *BEST* answers the question or completes the statement. *PRINT THE LETTER OF THE CORRECT ANSWER IN THE SPACE AT THE RIGHT.*

1. What is the purpose of state regulation of real estate salesmen and brokers?

    A. To insure that all brokers and salesmen have the same or equivalent credentials.
    B. To make certain that the state has a record of everyone in this profession.
    C. To protect dealers in real estate from unlicensed persons who act as brokers and to protect the public from inept or dishonest persons.
    D. To make it easier for real estate to be sold.

2. Which of the following is *NOT* a proper subject for a real estate salesman to handle?

    A. A burial plot
    B. A mortgage
    C. The rental on a summer cottage
    D. The collection of rent

3. The state regulates the real estate profession by authority of

    A. its interest in the land
    B. eminent domain
    C. its police power
    D. its taxing power

4. "Real estate," as used in the profession, means

    A. only interests in the land
    B. only fee simple interests
    C. tenements
    D. tenements, hereditaments, and all interests in land

5. Which of the following is a real estate broker?

    A. A real estate gallery which lists property and secures a fee for such listings
    B. A broker who negotiates the purchase and sale of bonds and other securities based upon real estate mortgages but who does not negotiate the loan which gives rise to the security
    C. A janitor or superintendent who collects rents and is employed by the owner of the building
    D. All of the above

6. A person, co-partnership, or corporation can engage in or hold itself out as a real estate broker or salesman

    A. at all times provided there is no sale if not licensed
    B. at all times when an application for a license is pending
    C. As long as his employer or partner has a license
    D. only if he, himself, is licensed

7. A real estate broker must be   7._____

   A. 21 years old to be eligible for a license
   B. 18 years old to be eligible for a license
   C. a high school graduate
   D. a college graduate

8. A real estate salesman must be   8._____

   A. 21 years old to be eligible for a license
   B. 18 years old to be eligible for a license
   C. a high school graduate
   D. a college graduate

9. A real estate broker must   9._____

   A. be a United States citizen to be licensed
   B. have declared his intention of becoming a citizen of the United States
   C. have declared his intention of becoming a United States citizen and actually have become one within 7 years or suffer revocation of his license or refusal to renew
   D. be a resident of the United States for 10 years

10. A broker's or salesman's license will NOT be given to a person   10._____

    A. who has been convicted of a felony anywhere in the United States
    B. who has been convicted of a felony in the licensing state only
    C. who has been convicted of a felony anywhere in the United States and if such offense is cognizable as a felony in the licensing state as well
    D. none of the above

11. A person who has been convicted of a felony so as to be ineligible for a broker's or salesman's license   11._____

    A. may never get a license
    B. must wait ten years to be eligible
    C. must petition the state licensing board to be eligible
    D. will be eligible subsequent to conviction if he has received an executive pardon or a certificate of good conduct from a parole board

12. An application for a broker's license would MOST surely be turned down if the Division of Licenses in the Department of State believed that   12._____

    A. the applicant could not write well in English
    B. the applicant is untrustworthy
    C. the applicant did not graduate from college
    D. the applicant was never a real estate salesman

13. Which of the following is NOT a mandatory requirement for an applicant for a broker's license?   13._____

    A. Knowledge of the English language
    B. Knowledge of deeds, mortgages, land contracts of sale, leases
    C. Experience as a licensed real estate salesman for at least two years
    D. A determination of the applicant's trustworthy nature

14. Which of the following is NOT an alternative qualification for obtaining a broker's license?

    A. Active participation in the real estate brokerage business as a licensed salesman for 2 years
    B. General experience in brokerage business for 2 years
    C. Active participation in general real estate brokerage business as a licensed salesman for at least one year and attendance for at least 45 hours on a real estate course approved by the Secretary of State
    D. A voucher by a real estate broker that the applicant is competent in this field

15. Legal title to real estate passes when

    A. a duly executed deed is delivered to the buyer
    B. the deed is properly signed
    C. the deed is notarized and sealed
    D. the deed is recorded

16. In order to accurately ascertain the CORRECT boundaries of real property, one should obtain a(n)

    A. title policy
    B. survey
    C. abstract
    D. warranty deed

17. The person who conveys title to real estate is called the

    A. grantee
    B. trustee
    C. grantor
    D. executor

18. Title to real estate is conveyed when

    A. the act of sale is recorded
    B. the act of sale is signed by the parties
    C. copy of the act of sale is received
    D. parties agree to sell to buyer

19. Title to fixtures, shelves, counters and merchandise is transferred or conveyed by if the

    A. deed
    B. bill of sale
    C. security agreement
    D. escrow

20. The rights of a person who owns a property but has leased it to someone else are referred to as _____ estate.

    A. lessee's
    B. fee simple
    C. leasehold
    D. leased fee

21. Untrue statements made on an application for either a broker's or salesman's license   21.____

    A. must be corrected within 30 days
    B. don't matter since the department will check each answer any way
    C. will be punished by taking away the license
    D. will be adjudged as perjury and treated as such

22. All of the following statements about deeds are true EXCEPT: 22.____

    A. A deed must be in writing
    B. Delivery of a deed takes place whether or not the physical paper leaves the possession of the grantor
    C. If the grantor gives the deed to the grantee, a valid delivery has been executed, regardless of the intention of the grantor
    D. A deed is duly executed when it is signed and intended to operate as such by the grantor

23. An applicant who does NOT apply for renewal within the specified time   23.____

    A. may never receive a renewal
    B. may ask for special dispensation upon appropriate grounds
    C. may qualify by taking the written examination
    D. receives a renewal as a matter of right

24. The license of a real estate salesman is kept by   24.____

    A. the license department
    B. the salesman
    C. the broker who employs the salesman
    D. all of the above

25. If a salesman voluntarily leaves his job,   25.____

    A. the salesman's license must be returned to the department
    B. the salesman must take the license with him to his next employer
    C. the former employer must keep the license on file for one year
    D. the salesman must get a photostat of his license to take with him

KEY (CORRECT ANSWERS)

1.	C	11.	D
2.	A	12.	B
3.	C	13.	C
4.	D	14.	D
5.	A	15.	A
6.	D	16.	B
7.	A	17.	C
8.	B	18.	B
9.	C	19.	A
10.	C	20.	D

21. D
22. C
23. C
24. C
25. A

———

TEST 2

DIRECTIONS: Each question or incomplete statement is followed by several suggested answers or completions. Select the one that BEST answers the question or completes the statement. PRINT THE LETTER OF THE CORRECT ANSWER IN THE SPACE AT THE RIGHT.

1. After a salesman has voluntarily left his job for another company and his employer returns his license to the department, 1.____

   A. the salesman must requalify for the license
   B. the department will forthwith re-issue the license
   C. the salesman must pay $1 and submit written notification of new employment to have his license re-issued
   D. The salesman need only submit the name and address of his new employer-broker

2. A purchaser of real property, all other things being equal, would prefer to have a 2.____

   A. warranty deed
   B. quitclaim deed
   C. bargain and sale deed without covenant against grantor
   D. referee's deed

3. Which of the following is a FALSE statement? 3.____

   A. Each licensed broker shall have and maintain a definite place of business within the state.
   B. Each licensed broker shall conspicuously post on the outside of the building or in some other suitable place the words "licensed real estate broker."
   C. Each licensed broker shall be required to display his license only in his main office, not in his branch offices.
   D. Each licensed broker shall display as many licenses as he has officers.

4. Licenses issued to real estate brokers 4.____

   A. must be conspicuously displayed
   B. must be available upon request
   C. must be on file with company records
   D. must be put on the front door of each office

5. A change in business address by a licensee 5.____

   A. must be inserted in colored ink on the license by the licensee
   B. is to be ignored until the licensee applies for a renewal of his license
   C. must be telephoned to the department of licenses for its records
   D. must be given to the department in writing, whereupon the department shall issue a new license upon return of the original license and pocket card and payment

6. A change in address by a licensee without notification and re-issue 6.____

   A. makes the licensee guilty of perjury
   B. annuls the license
   C. makes the licensee ineligible for renewal
   D. has no legal effect

7. A pocket card shall be issued by the department to each licensed broker or salesman

   A. on demand
   B. on payment of a fee
   C. as a matter of law
   D. in special cases

8. A pocket card is

   A. like a business card
   B. an evidence of insurance
   C. like a certificate
   D. is an extra used to impress clients

9. The pocket card

   A. must be prominently displayed by the broker or salesman at all times
   B. must be kept with company records
   C. must be given to each client
   D. must be shown on demand

10. A warranty deed

    A. must be specified in the contract for sale of the property
    B. is assumed if no type of deed is specified
    C. is an option open to the grantee after the contract is closed
    D. is an extraordinary type of deed

11. In terms of a deed, the grantee is the

    A. title company
    B. buyer
    C. broker
    D. seller

12. The re-issuance of a license

    A. requires a new certificate to be issued
    B. permits the department to endorse a license and pocket card previously issued
    C. requires that the department state in a conspicuous place on the certificate how many renewals have been made
    D. requires none of the above

13. The death of a real estate broker who was at the time of his death the sole proprietor of a brokerage office

    A. revokes the broker's license as of the date of death
    B. has no effect on the others in the office
    C. permits the decedent's administrator or executor to complete any unfinished transactions for a 120-day period
    D. gives all salesmen and the decedent's administrator 120 days to transact new, as well as complete unfinished, business

14. Which of the following is a good information resource for those seeking information about abutters to a property?

    A. Registry of probate
    B. Registry of deeds
    C. Genealogical library
    D. Town assessor's office

15. The *riparian doctrine* in real estate is concerned with

    A. the government's right to take possession of property
    B. water rights
    C. land boundary settlement
    D. proximity to the nearest running stream or river

16. The information in most older recorded deeds, including names and signatures, comprises

    A. originals   B. abstracts   C. transcriptions   D. extracts

17. Which of the following is a term used for an adjoining neighbor in many deed records?

    A. Associate   B. Abstracter   C. Adjacent   D. Abutter

18. A broker's license issued to a corporation entitles

    A. all officers of the corporation to act as a real estate broker
    B. only the secretary of the corporation to act as a real estate broker
    C. only the president to act as a real estate broker
    D. none of the above

19. A member of a co-partnership or corporation licensed as a real estate broker

    A. does not have to pay an additional license fee for his license if he is not the president of the corporation
    B. cannot get a real estate salesman's license
    C. can always apply for a real estate salesman's license
    D. pays only half as much as the corporation or co-partnership for his license

20. An individual real estate broker who becomes an officer of a corporation

    A. may have his license endorsed by the department so that he may act as the corporation's representative
    B. must pay for a new license but does not have to take the test again
    C. must wait for the term of his license to expire before the corporation applies for a license for him
    D. may have his license endorsed by the board of directors so that he may act as the corporation's representative

21. What is the specific term for the conveyance of a future interest in real property by the person holding that interest to the person holding the prior possessory interest?

    A. Reversion   B. Surrender   C. Remainder   D. Release

22. Which of the following is grounds for suspension or revocation by the department of state of a broker's license?

    A. Conviction of violation of a rule
    B. Material misstatement in the application for a license
    C. Incompetency
    D. All of the above

23. After a broker's license has been revoked or suspended, which of these circumstances may result?
    1. The license may be displayed pending an appeal.
    2. The license must not be displayed.
    3. The license must be returned to the department of state.
    4. The license may be held in escrow by an attorney or a bank.

    The CORRECT combination is:

    A. 1, 3   B. 2, 4   C. 1, 4   D. 2, 3

24. When a broker's or salesman's license is revoked by the department, the broker or salesman   24.____

    A. can never be re-licensed
    B. must petition the department within 6 months to be relicensed
    C. cannot be relicensed until after the expiration of one year
    D. cannot be relicensed until after the expiration of five years

25. How can a broker's "untrustworthiness" be shown? By   25.____

    A. proof of racial discrimination in renting or selling
    B. proof of placement of "blind ads"
    C. failure to indicate "dealer" in an advertisement
    D. all of the above

KEY (CORRECT ANSWERS)

1.	C	11.	B
2.	A	12.	B
3.	C	13.	C
4.	A	14.	D
5.	D	15.	B
6.	B	16.	C
7.	C	17.	D
8.	B	18.	C
9.	D	19.	B
10.	A	20.	A

21.	D
22.	D
23.	D
24.	C
25.	D

TEST 3

DIRECTIONS: Each question or incomplete statement is followed by several suggested answers or completions. Select the one that *BEST* answers the question or completes the statement. *PRINT THE LETTER OF THE CORRECT ANSWER IN THE SPACE AT THE RIGHT.*

1. The revocation of a broker's license

   A. has no effect on the validity of the licenses of his salesmen
   B. has no effect on the validity of the licenses of his salesmen if they find new employment with a licensed broker within one month
   C. suspends the licenses of his salesmen until they find new employment and get new licenses
   D. revokes the licenses of his salesmen as well

   1.____

2. If his employer-broker license has been revoked,

   A. the salesman-employee must pay for a new license in order to work for a new, employer
   B. the salesman-employee will be issued a new license without charge
   C. the samesman-employee must only pay half the cost of the original license
   D. none of the above, or all of the above

   2.____

3. The department of state, before denying an application for license or before revoking or suspending any license or imposing any find or reprimand on the holder,

   A. shall call the applicant or licensee and tell him of the charges against him
   B. shall subpoena the applicant or licensee to appear
   C. shall notify in writing the applicant or licensee of the charges against him at least 20 days prior to the date set for hearing
   D. none of the above, or all of the above

   3.____

4. At a hearing to determine whether a license should be revoked or an application denied,

   A. the applicant or licensee must appear in person
   B. the applicant or licensee must be represented by counsel
   C. the applicant or licensee must appear with counsel
   D. the applicant or licensee has a choice whether to appear in person or be represented by counsel

   4.____

5. Which of the following concerning the notice of the charges and the hearing are *TRUE*? It
   1. may be served by delivery to the applicant or licensee
   2. may be served by registered mail to the last known business address of the licensee
   3. shall also be given to the broker-employer if the charges are against a salesman
   4. shall be contained in a subpoena and served personally on the licensee

   The *CORRECT* combination is:

   A. 1, 2   B. 4 only   C. 1, 2, 3   D. 1, 2, 3, 4

   5.____

6. The department

   A. can suspend a license pending a hearing
   B. cannot suspend a license until the hearing has ascertained the licensee's guilt
   C. can hold the licensee in contempt until it has determined his innocence or guilt
   D. has a choice of any one of the above alternatives

7. What is the term for land rights based on occupation, rather than conveyance?

   A. Adverse claim
   B. Domain
   C. Easement appurtenant
   D. Indentured jurisdiction

8. The granting or the refusal to grant a license or renewal and the imposition of a fine or reprimand or the refusal to impose a fine or reprimand

   A. is final
   B. is subject to the review of the courts
   C. is subject to review by the Attorney General
   D. can only be questioned by the license holder or applicant

9. Which of the following is a *TRUE* statement?

   A. A broker may never split a commission with another broker.
   B. A broker cannot split a commission with a broker from another state.
   C. A broker can split his commission with whoever deserves a part thereof.
   D. A broker can split his commission with a licensed salesman

10. A broker *CANNOT*

    A. split his commission with a broker from another state
    B. split his commission with a party to the transaction
    C. split his commission with a licensed salesman
    D. split his commission

11. Which of the following is *FALSE?*

    A. A real estate broker cannot offer prizes for names of prospective customers.
    B. Payment for names of prospective customers does not violate a rule.
    C. An unlicensed broker cannot recover a fee for his aid from a licensed broker.
    D. A broker may share a commission with a broker licensed in another state although he is not licensed in this state.

12. A real estate salesman

    A. may be paid only by his employer
    B. may demand a fee from the party for whom he negotiated the transaction in lieu of his commission due from his employer
    C. may get both a fee from the interested party and from his employer
    D. may get a fee for appraising real estate

13. When a broker discharges a salesman,

A. the broker must send the salesman's license to the department of state with a sworn statement as to the reason why the salesman was discharged
B. the broker need not report the discharge since the salesman's new employer must report the salesman as a new employee
C. the salesman must send his license in to the department of state
D. the department will ascertain the salesman's new position during its annual investigation of broker's offices

14. When a broker discharges a salesman, 14._____

    A. the salesman will not find out about it until the department of state notifies him
    B. the broker must verbally make it clear to the salesman why he was discharged
    C. the broker must mail the salesman a communication that his license has been returned and a copy of that communication must be attached to the salesman's license when it is returned
    D. the salesman must verify to the department that he had notice from his broker that his license had been returned

15. When the salesman's employment is mutually terminated or he voluntarily terminates his own employment, 15._____

    A. the salesman shall return his license to the department
    B. the salesman shall write to the department the reason why he left the broker's employ
    C. the broker shall send the salesman's license to the department with the reason for the termination of employment attached
    D. none of the above

16. Upon termination of the salesman's employment, 16._____

    A. the broker must send his own license to the department along with that of the salesman
    B. the broker must send his pocket card to the department
    C. the salesman must send his license to the department
    D. the salesman must send his pocket card to the department

17. A real estate salesman may work for a new employer 17._____

    A. immediately, pending the issuance of a new license
    B. immediately, but cannot get a commission until he gets his license
    C. only after the employer gets his license from the department
    D. only if the salesman agrees to his commissions being held in escrow until he gets his license

18. A broker 18._____

    A. bears the responsibility for any wrongdoing of his employees
    B. bears the responsibility for only those acts of his employees done in the course of their employment
    C. can have his license suspended or revoked if he knows that his employee has committed a wrongdoing or keeps the profits thereof
    D. is not responsible for any wrongdoing of his employees unless he, himself, took an active part therein

19. If an unlicensed salesman or a salesman without a temporary permit works for a licensed broker,

    A. the salesman is guilty of a misdemeanor
    B. the broker is guilty of a misdemeanor
    C. the salesman is guilty of a felony
    D. the salesman can work until he gets his license

    19.____

20. In order to bring or maintain a court action for compensation for services rendered,

    A. a salesman or broker must prove his part in the transaction
    B. a salesman or broker must state and prove that he was duly licensed on the date the action allegedly arose
    C. a salesman or broker must prove that he is duly licensed on the date of trial
    D. the defendant must prove that the salesman or broker was not licensed on the date of the action

    20.____

21. Which of the following is *FALSE?*

    A. A transaction by an unlicensed broker is unlawful and an assignee acquires no enforceable rights under such contract to pay commission.
    B. Where only one of two co-brokers engaged in the sale or lease of property is duly licensed, neither broker is entitled to recover for his services.
    C. A real estate broker is entitled to a commission arising from the sale of real estate where he was not a licensed broker at the time he obtained a purchaser since he was not to be paid his commission until title had passed and since he had obtained his license between the time he procured the purchaser and the time title passed.
    D. Commissions lawfully earned by a duly licensed real estate salesman do not cease to be payable to him by reason of a change in his employment before he has received same.

    21.____

22. A violation of any provision of a rule is a

    A. misdemeanor
    B. felony
    C. misdemeanor or felony depending upon which provision is violated
    D. perjury

    22.____

23. The highest form of an estate, under which the owner can use the property at will and depose of it without restriction, is

    A. leasehold
    B. fee simple
    C. leased fee
    D. life estate

    23.____

24. A violation of a provision is committed when

    A. the intent of the provision is defied
    B. a single act which is prohibited is committed
    C. someone is hurt by the commission of the prohibited act
    D. a series of wrongful deeds produces an unjust enrichment for the broker

    24.____

25. Ideally, a title chain developed during a search should go back at least to the	25.____
   A. very first owner of the parcel
   B. developer of the subdivision
   C. first owner after the initial subdivision
   D. last known owner

KEY (CORRECT ANSWERS)

1. C	11. A
2. B	12. A
3. C	13. A
4. D	14. C
5. C	15. C
6. A	16. D
7. A	17. C
8. B	18. C
9. D	19. B
10. B	20. B

21. C
22. A
23. B
24. B
25. B

TEST 4

DIRECTIONS: Each question or incomplete statement is followed by several suggested answers or completions. Select the one that BEST answers the question or completes the statement. PRINT THE LETTER OF THE CORRECT ANSWER IN THE SPACE AT THE RIGHT.

1. An offender who has received any sum of money as commission, compensation, or profit as a consequence of his violation   1._____

    A. shall be liable for exactly the amount he wrongly received
    B. shall be liable for not more than half the amount he wrongly received
    C. shall be held liable for four times the amount he wrongly received
    D. may be held liable up to four times the amount he wrongly received

2. What is the term for the voluntary conveyance of title to land from an individual private owner to a public agency?   2._____

    A. Dedication
    B. Accretion
    C. Escheat
    D. Accession

3. Which of the following statements is TRUE regarding both liens and easements? They   3._____

    A. must be recorded in public land records to be legal
    B. are both encumbrances
    C. may be imposed against the property only after all parties involved have agreed
    D. must be in writing to be legal

4. What is the term for an improvement or object, such as a building or driveway, that extends across the legal boundary of an adjoining tract of land?   4._____

    A. Lien
    B. Encroachment
    C. Encumbrance
    D. Easement

5. In a prosecution for a wrong allegedly done by a real estate broker,   5._____

    A. the broker must prove beyond a shadow of a doubt that the other party agreed to pay him the commission he was given
    B. the aggrieved party must allege and prove that there was an agreement to pay the broker but it was bad
    C. it is presumed that any broker who offers to negotiate a sale of real estate for another is doing so for a fee
    D. none of the above

6. A real estate transaction is presumed to be done for a commission   6._____

    A. whenever one goes to a broker for his professional advice
    B. whenever a broker completes a transaction which benefits a private
    C. whenever the broker performs repeated and successive acts, offers or attempts, and can prove the same
    D. all of the above

7. Who has the power to enforce the provisions of licensing statutes?   7._____

   A. Secretary of State B. Attorney General
   C. District Attorney D. All of the above

8. Violations of licensing statutes and rules   8._____

   A. are investigated on complaint of any person
   B. are investigated on the initiative of the officer in charge
   C. are investigated on the initiative of the officer in charge and/or on the complaint of any person
   D. are investigated by the Grand Jury

9. The investigative powers   9._____

   A. are limited to the alleged violations
   B. extend to the alleged violations, business practices and methods of the company
   C. extend to the alleged violations, business practices and methods of the company, and any other related item within the discretion of the investigating officer
   D. are limited by the warrant used by the officer

10. The investigation   10._____

    A. is limited to the pertinent data surrounding the alleged violation
    B. is all-inclusive, and any information must be supplied on request by the licensee
    C. does not permit the investigatory officer to ask personal or non-business questions, since this is a violation of the First Amendment
    D. none of the above

11. A person under investigation   11._____

    A. can be subpoenaed to appear
    B. must be given a month's notice of the date of his appearance
    C. can only be subpoenaed if he is the owner of the business
    D. can be subpoenaed only if he is to appear in his own county

12. A person under investigation   12._____

    A. is under oath when he gives testimony
    B. is not under oath when he gives testimony since this is not a court of law
    C. is on his honor to tell the truth
    D. none of the above

13. A person who does NOT appear when subpoenaed   13._____

    A. suffers no penalty if he comes the second time
    B. is given 30 days to defend himself
    C. is guilty of a misdemeanor
    D. may be guilty of a misdemeanor if he has no valid excuse

14. A person who refuses to answer a question when his deposition is being taken   14._____

    A. is guilty of a misdemeanor
    B. is guilty of a misdemeanor depending upon the question

C. is guilty of a misdemeanor if he has no valid reason for not answering
D. is guilty of a violation of the Fifth Amendment

15. During an investigation for alleged violation, 15.____

    A. the person must answer each and every question at his peril at all times
    B. the person being investigated can be given an immunity from prosecution by the presiding official if he answers questions put to him which may incriminate him
    C. the person being investigated must be given immunity before he can answer any questions
    D. the person being investigated is only entitled to be given an immunity if he is in criminal court

16. Which of the following statements is *FALSE?* 16.____

    A. An attorney at law is not required to be licensed in order to act as a real estate broker.
    B. An attorney who is not licensed as a real estate broker may act as co-broker with a licensed real estate broker and share the brokerage compensation.
    C. Salesmen employed by an attorney who acts as a real estate broker do not have to be licensed.
    D. Any public officer or a person acting under court order does not have to be licensed to act as a real estate broker.

17. An attorney who deals exclusively in real estate 17.____

    A. must have a real estate broker's license
    B. does not need a license
    C. can recover the commission for someone who is unlicensed as an assignee
    D. and has a license can no longer act as a broker if his license is revoked

18. A non-resident real estate broker 18.____

    A. shall be required to maintain a place of business in this state
    B. must maintain a place of business in this state if he does not maintain a definite place of business in another state
    C. cannot act as a real estate broker in this state unless he is licensed by this state
    D. is not required to maintain a place of business in this state regardless of whether or not he has a definite place of business in another state

19. A non-resident real estate broker 19.____

    A. must take the examination and obtain a license to act in this state
    B. can act in this state without a license
    C. only needs a license to act in this state if his own state requires licensed non-residents to get a license in that state
    D. does not need a license although his resident state requires non-residents to get a state license

20. If the non-resident is licensed in another state but that state does not require a written examination,

    A. he must pay the license fee to get a license from this state
    B. he must pay the license fee and submit a certified copy of the non-state license to get a license from this state
    C. he must take this state's written examination, pay the license fee and submit a copy of his license to get a license from this state
    D. he does not have to do anything to get a license from this state other than submit a copy of his non-state license

21. Every non-resident, upon filing an application for a license or renewal,

    A. shall state his address and main place of business
    B. shall file an irrevocable consent to be sued in this state by submitting himself to the jurisdiction of the state courts
    C. waives the right to be sued in this state
    D. retains the right to be sued in his home state and cannot be sued in any other state

22. In a suit by a resident against a non-resident real estate broker,

    A. the plaintiff must hire a deputy to personally serve the non-resident when he is in the plaintiff's state
    B. the plaintiff must hire a deputy to personally serve the non-resident in his home state
    C. the plaintiff can either serve the secretary of state personally or by registered mail, and must enclose a specified fee
    D. the plaintiff must serve the secretary of state personally and must enclose a fee

23. How is a non-resident broker or salesman notified of a suit against him? By

    A. personal service of process by the plaintiff when he is in the plaintiff's state
    B. registered mail from the plaintiff to the non-resident's out-of-state office
    C. notification from the department of state
    D. registered mail from the secretary of state of the plaintiff's state

24. Each non-resident broker or salesman

    A. must carry his home state's pocket card to show on request in this state
    B. must carry a pocket card issued by the department of state of this state which is distinguishable from that of resident brokers and salesmen
    C. must carry a pocket card issued by the department of state of this state which is a different color than that of resident brokers and salesmen
    D. does not have to carry a pocket card since he is not a resident of this state

25. Which of the following statements is *FALSE?*

    A. The secretary of state can appoint five brokers and five salesmen to an advisory committee to help the department to administer and enforce this article.
    B. The department of state enforces rules.
    C. The advisory committee serves without compensation.
    D. The employees of the department of state who handle real estate affairs are payed according to the civil service law.

KEY (CORRECT ANSWERS)

1. D
2. A
3. B
4. B
5. C

6. C
7. A
8. C
9. C
10. B

11. A
12. A
13. D
14. C
15. B

16. C
17. A
18. B
19. C
20. C

21. B
22. C
23. D
24. C
25. A

TEST 5

DIRECTIONS: Each question or incomplete statement is followed by several suggested answers or completions. Select the one that BEST answers the question or completes the statement. PRINT THE LETTER OF THE CORRECT ANSWER IN THE SPACE AT THE RIGHT.

1. Which combination of the following statements is FALSE?
   1. The real estate commission may, on its own motion, investigate any action of a licensee and call the matter for a hearing.
   2. The real estate commission may revoke a broker's license as well as a salesman's license if the salesman is found guilty of conduct of fraudulent or dishonest dealing.
   3. A friend of a broker, not in any way connected with the real estate business, may receive a bonus or a gift, as long as it is not a stated or computed commission, for assisting in making a deal.
   4. A person who was licensed five years ago and has been inactive for two years may, upon application, secure a license for the current year without taking an examination.

   The CORRECT combination is:

   A. 1, 2, 3, 4   B. 3, 4   C. 1, 4   D. 2, 4

2. Which combination of the following statements is FALSE?
   1. A real estate broker should keep his license in a safety deposit vault or other safe place so that it cannot be lost or stolen.
   2. A salesman may split a commission with any other licensed salesman or broker.
   3. It is lawful for a salesman to complete a deal, collect the commission in his own name, and then give his broker his agreed share.
   4. A real estate salesman can collect, in his own name, money in connection with a real estate transaction.

   The CORRECT combination is:

   A. none of the above   B. all of the above
   C. 2, 3, 4   D. 4 only

3. Which combination of the following statements is TRUE?
   1. A broker is required to notify the Real Estate Commission immediately after a salesman leaves his employ.
   2. It is not a violation of law for a broker to pay a commission directly to a salesman employed by another broker.
   3. It is a violation of the real estate license law for a salesman or broker to offer as an inducement to enter into a contract for the purchase or sale of real estate anything of value other than the consideration recited in the sales contract.
   4. A real estate broker must notify the real estate commission in writing immediately upon receipt of notice from the surety that the surety has made payment on the broker's bond.

   The CORRECT combination is:

   A. 1, 3, 4   B. 1, 3   C. 3, 4   D. 1, 2, 3, 4

4. Which combination of the following statements is *FALSE*?
    1. A broker must immediately notify the real estate commission when he changes his business address.
    2. The owner of a business lot sold it at a figure approximately twice its cost. In showing the adjoining lot to a prospective buyer, a real estate broker is entirely within his rights to make a definite promise of a similar profit to his customer.
    3. A salesman may not sue anyone except his broker for the collection of a real estate commission.
    4. A licensed salesman may divide his commission with another licensed salesman with a broker's consent.

    The *CORRECT* combination is:

    A. 1, 2   B. 2, 3, 4   C. 1, 2, 3, 4   D. 3, 4

5. Which combination of the following statements is *TRUE*?
    1. A person who sells a parcel of real estate under a court order is not required to have a license.
    2. Assessments are for the support of the Government.
    3. Escrow is another name for a husband's interest in his wife's property.
    4. The real estate commission may refuse to issue, revoke, or suspend a license immediately upon receiving a serious complaint against a broker or salesman.

    The *CORRECT* combination is:

    A. 1, 4   B. 1, 2   C. 2 only   D. 1 only

6. Which combination of the following statements is *FALSE*?
    1. A broker who knows that misrepresentations are being made by his salesmen may have his license revoked, even though he, himself, is not guilty of making any misrepresentations.
    2. A broker accepting a net listing to sell a piece of real estate should not accept any compensation from the purchaser unless he reveals this fact to the seller.
    3. It is not necessary for a person to hold a real estate license to execute, buy, or sell an option.
    4. A broker may sell his own personal property to a client without disclosing that fact.

    The *CORRECT* combination is:

    A. 3, 4   B. 1, 4   C. 2, 3   D. 1, 2, 3

7. Which combination of the following statements is *TRUE*?
    1. An applicant for a salesman's license must be a citizen of the United States.
    2. Complete and accurate records of real estate transactions need not be kept by the broker, if the deal is satisfactorily closed.
    3. The salesman should open a separate account for the deposits he receives.
    4. A salesman must include the name of his broker in his advertisements.

    The *CORRECT* combination is:

    A. 1, 2, 4   B. 1, 4   C. 2, 4   D. 1, 3, 4

8. Which combination of the following statements is *FALSE*?
   1. It is necessary that a licensed real estate broker shall erect a sign where he has his office on which shall be plainly stated that he is a licensed real estate broker.
   2. Either the salesman or the broker must witness the contract.
   3. A broker must be the procuring cause to be entitled to a commission on an open listing.
   4. Revocation of the broker's license automatically suspends the salesman's license.

   The *CORRECT* combination is:

   A. 1, 2   B. 3, 4   C. 2 only   D. 2, 4

9. Which combination of the following statements is *FALSE*?
   1. The filing of an application for a license allows the applicant to operate.
   2. If you, a salesman for Broker A, with your Broker's consent, make a deal with Broker B, then, Broker B, knowing you are licensed, can pay you your earned portion of the commission.
   3. If a broker thinks there will be future profits from the resale of property he is selling, he may so guarantee them to his client.
   4. A licensed salesman may go to work for another broker immediately upon the filing of a request for transfer.

   The *CORRECT* combination is:

   A. 1, 3, 4   B. 1, 2, 3, 4   C. 1, 4   D. 3, 4

10. Which combination of the following statements is *FALSE*?
    1. Each branch office of a broker must be in the charge of a licensed broker or salesman.
    2. All listings secured by a salesman belong to the broker.
    3. A real estate salesman should carry his license at all times to properly identify himself.
    4. A real estate salesman must turn all deposits over to his broker.

    The *CORRECT* combination is:

    A. 1, 3   B. 3, 4   C. 1, 3, 4   D. 3 only

11. Which combination of the following statements is *TRUE*?
    1. One real estate transaction requires a license.
    2. The real estate commission has the power to subpoena records in real estate transactions.
    3. Failure to give a buyer a copy of the offer he signs is reason for the revocation of a real estate license.
    4. An employee who only solicits listings need not be licensed.

    The *CORRECT* combination is:

    A. 1, 2   B. 1, 2, 3   C. 2, 3, 4   D. 1, 3, 4

12. What is the purpose of the law governing real estate brokers and salesmen?
    1. To define the business of real estate brokers and real estate salesmen.
    2. To regulate and supervise the activities of all those engaged in the real estate business as brokers and salesmen.
    3. To require those engaged in such business to have licenses.
    4. To provide methods for the issuance, revocation, and suspension of such licenses.
    5. To protect the general public against unscrupulous brokers and salesmen.

    The CORRECT combination is:

    A. 1, 3, 5
    B. 1, 2, 3, 4
    C. 1, 4
    D. all of the above

13. Which combination of the following statements is TRUE?
    1. Everyone engaged in the business of real property management requires a license as a broker or salesman.
    2. One act as a real estate broker or salesman will require a person engaged in such business to take out a license.
    3. An applicant for a broker's license is not required to file a bond.
    4. An applicant for a real estate license may not engage in the real estate business until the license is in his possession or in the possession of the broker and has been registered with the clerk of the court.

    The CORRECT combination is:

    A. 1, 2
    B. 3 only
    C. 1, 4
    D. 1, 2, 4

14. The purpose of posting a bond in connection with the application for a real estate broker's license is
    1. to ensure the faithful observance of all the provisions of the law
    2. to make it difficult for the financially insecure to become real estate brokers
    3. that the bond shall indemnify any person who may be damaged by a failure on the part of an applicant for a real estate license to conduct his business in accordance with the requirements of the license law
    4. to give the government another source of revenue

15. Which combination of the following statements is FALSE?
    1. Before a client signs a purchase agreement, the broker or salesman has a positive duty to explain the agreement in detail.
    2. Upon receipt of the licenses by the broker, he must register them with the clerk of courts or display them in his place of business.
    3. Immediately upon the termination of the association of a real estate salesman with his broker, the broker shall return the salesman's license to the real estate commission for cancellation.
    4. In case of any change of business location, the broker must notify the real estate commission and return his license to the commission, whereupon a new license will be issued.

    The CORRECT combination is:

    A. 1, 2
    B. 3, 4
    C. 2 only
    D. 1, 2, 4

16. Which of the following activities are NOT lawfully allowed to be performed by a licensed real estate salesman?   16._____
    1. Transact any real estate brokerage business in his own name
    2. Open and maintain a branch office in his own name
    3. Employ salesmen
    4. Advertise and list, using his own name
    5. Close deals
    The CORRECT combination is:

    A. all of the above   B. 1, 4   C. 5 only   D. 3, 4, 5

17. Which combination of the following statements is TRUE?   17._____
    1. If a real estate license is not registered with the clerk of courts, it is invalid.
    2. A real estate broker is liable for frauds and misrepresentations of any salesman associated with him, even where the broker has no knowledge of the misrepresentation.
    3. A real estate salesman may receive compensation from any broker with whom he has dealings.
    4. The salesman must keep his license in his personal possession.
    The CORRECT combination is:

    A. 1 only   B. 1, 2   C. 1, 2, 3   D. 4 only

18. Which combination of the following statements is FALSE?   18._____
    1. It is unnecessary to register your license.
    2. You must be an American citizen to obtain a broker's or salesman's license.
    3. The division of commission between a broker and his salesman is determined by their agreement.
    4. A salesman may engage in the real estate business before his license is received from the commission.
    The CORRECT combination is:

    A. 1, 2   B. 2, 3   C. 1, 4   D. 1, 2, 4

19. Which combination of the following statements is FALSE?   19._____
    1. Attorneys are exempt from the real estate license law requirements.
    2. A person who gives only part of his time to the real estate business has to secure a license.
    3. An agreement of sale is simply one's consent that he intends to sell; a deed is evidence that he has bought and is now the owner of the property.
    4. The terms "real estate broker" and "Realtor" mean the same thing.
    The CORRECT combination is:

    A. 1, 2   B. 1, 2, 4   C. 1 only   D. 4 only

20. Which of the following are duties owed by a real estate broker to his client?   20._____
    1. To act for his client as he would if the property were his own.
    2. To treat fairly and without bias the person on the other side of the transaction.
    3. To offer property solely on its merit without exaggeration, concealment, or misrepresentation.
    4. To protect the public against fraud or unethical practices.
    The CORRECT combination is:

    A. 2, 3   B. 2 only   C. 2, 3, 4   D. all of the above

21. Which combination of the following statements is *FALSE*?
    1. A real estate broker may never receive compensation from both parties to a sale or trade.
    2. The terms "realty," "real estate," and "real property" are interchangeable.
    3. A deed conveying property to a creditor as security for the payment of a debt is called a mortgage.
    4. The code of ethics governs the conduct of licensed brokers and salesmen.
    The *CORRECT* combination is:

    A. 1 only
    B. 1,4
    C. 1,2
    D. none of the above

22. Which statements concerning the deposit are *TRUE*?
    1. The broker and the salesman may split the deposit according to their agreement.
    2. The deposit is part of the purchase price paid by the buyer.
    3. Neither the broker nor the salesman has the right to the deposit.
    4. The seller pays for the services of the broker -- the buyer's deposit is to the seller.
    The *CORRECT* statements are:

    A. 1, 2, 4   B. 1, 4   C. 2, 3   D. 2, 3, 4

23. Which combination of the following statements is *TRUE*?
    1. If a salesman is personally convinced that a certain piece of property will increase in value, he can lawfully guarantee a future profit to the prospective purchaser.
    2. A real estate broker is one employed for negotiating the sale, purchase, or exchange of real estate for a commission contingent on success.
    3. A real estate salesman is one employed by a broker to procure a sale, purchase, or exchange of real estate.
    4. The holding of a salesman's license authorizes the licensee to list or advertise property in his own name.
    The *CORRECT* combination is:

    A. 2, 3   B. 1, 2, 3   C. 2, 3, 4   D. 1, 2, 3, 4

24. A real estate salesman is paid by the

    A. seller
    B. buyer
    C. broker to whom his license is issued
    D. escrow agent

25. A real estate salesman is entitled to receive

    A. 1/2 of the 5% commission
    B. what the broker decides is fair
    C. what he has earned, according to his agreement with the broker
    D. none of the above

KEY (CORRECT ANSWERS)

1.	B	11.	B
2.	B	12.	D
3.	A	13.	D
4.	B	14.	A
5.	D	15.	C
6.	A	16.	A
7.	B	17.	B
8.	C	18.	C
9.	B	19.	D
10.	D	20.	D

21. A
22. D
23. A
24. C
25. C

TEST 6

DIRECTIONS: Each question or incomplete statement is followed by several suggested answers or completions. Select the one that *BEST* answers the question or completes the statement. *PRINT THE LETTER OF THE CORRECT ANSWER IN THE SPACE AT THE RIGHT.*

1. Every real estate license *MUST* be registered at the

    A. office of the real estate commission
    B. local real estate board
    C. county clerk's office
    D. recorder's office

2. The license of a real estate broker or salesman may be revoked or suspended for violation of the real estate license law by

    A. the division of licenses and permits
    B. the court
    C. the National Association of real estate boards
    D. the state real estate commission

3. A licensed real estate salesman is permitted by law to represent

    A. several brokers
    B. only his employing broker
    C. himself as broker
    D. an interested third party

4. When a salesman is discharged or leaves the employ of a broker, the broker should

    A. give the salesman his license
    B. notify the local real estate board
    C. inform the salesman by telephone
    D. send the salesman's license to the real estate commission for cancellation, informing the salesman by letter, and sending a copy to the commission

5. To operate a branch office a broker *MUST*

    A. find a good location
    B. have his license endorsed to cover the branch office
    C. obtain a branch office license from the state real estate commission
    D. have 10 years' experience

6. A real estate salesman, upon receiving a deposit, should

    A. turn it over to the seller, less commission
    B. use it to cover expenses of the transaction
    C. give it to the broker to be placed in an escrow account
    D. give a party for the office staff

7. A copy of a broker's bond should be

    A. kept in a bank box
    B. displayed in the broker's office in public view
    C. kept in the office safe
    D. carried on the broker's person

8. Upon being sued in a real estate transaction, a salesman or broker should

    A. notify the state real estate commission
    B. leave the state
    C. effect a compromise
    D. declare bankruptcy

9. A salesman's license stays in the possession of

    A. the salesman
    B. the commission
    C. his broker
    D. his next of kin

10. Anyone operating in the real estate brokerage business without a license

    A. is subject to a fine and imprisonment
    B. is considered unethical
    C. is barred from ever getting a license
    D. cannot hire licensed salesmen

11. A broker should furnish a bond

    A. in an amount set by his state
    B. in his county of residence
    C. after he has been sued
    D. if he is insolvent

12. When a broker and salesman have a dispute over the commission, they should

    A. discuss it with buyer and seller
    B. each consult an attorney
    C. contact the real estate commission in writing
    D. request a hearing from the commission

13. The amount of commission to be paid a broker is fixed by

    A. statute law
    B. the department of occupational standards
    C. the state real estate commission
    D. agreement of the parties

14. To file a complaint against a licensed salesman or broker for one or more causes for revocation or suspension of a license, the complainant should

    A. telephone the state real estate commission
    B. write a letter to the department of occupational standards
    C. go to the commission to give an oral report of the details
    D. file the charges or complaint in affidavit form with the state real estate commission

15. To use the word "Realtor," a licensed broker MUST

    A. pass a written examination
    B. be issued a real estate license
    C. be an active member of a local real estate board
    D. be a member of the state commission

16. Unlicensed persons *CANNOT* legally collect a brokerage fee or commission because it is   16._____

    A. unethical
    B. against the rules of the local board
    C. not in the contract
    D. illegal

17. A corporation may engage in the real estate brokerage business only when the officer acting for the corporation   17._____

    A. is a duly licensed salesman
    B. has authority from the corporation commissioner
    C. is a licensed broker
    D. is the president of the corporation

18. The real estate law provides that all applicants for a real estate salesman's license *MUST* be   18._____

    A. a resident of the state for at least one year
    B. at least 21 years of age
    C. a citizen of the United States
    D. none of the above

19. Real property security dealers, who are required to file and maintain with the real estate commissioner a bond issued by an admitted corporate surety insurer, would have to file such a bond in the amount of   19._____

    A. $5,000   B. $7,500   C. $10,000   D. none of the above

20. A person who is engaged *SOLELY* in the appraisal of real estate is required to hold   20._____

    A. a real estate broker's license
    B. a real estate appraiser's license
    C. a membership card as a M.A.I.
    D. none of the above

21. Which of the following activities require a license in order to be performed by one on behalf of another for a stated compensation?   21._____
    1. To lease a summer house
    2. To offer to sell a bakery business
    3. To offer to exchange lands
    4. To appraise a going concern
    The *CORRECT* combination is:

    A. 1, 3   B. 1 only   C. 1, 4   D. all of the above

22. The term "compensation" includes   22._____

    A. salary   B. a fee
    C. commission   D. all of the above

23. The term "valuable consideration" includes

   A. only money consideration
   B. the granting of a favor
   C. anything of value
   D. all of the above

24. The term "real estate" refers to

   A. the land and all the buildings, fixtures, and improvements attached thereto
   B. the land only
   C. only buildings
   D. the land and all buildings only

25. Which of the following are "persons" within the meaning of the real estate law?
   1. Individuals
   2. Firms
   3. Co-partnerships
   4. Associations
   5. Corporations

   The CORRECT combination is:

   A. 1 only   B. 1, 5   C. 2, 5   D. 1, 2, 3, 4, 5

KEY (CORRECT ANSWERS)

1. C		11. A	
2. D		12. B	
3. B		13. D	
4. D		14. D	
5. C		15. C	
6. C		16. D	
7. B		17. C	
8. A		18. D	
9. C		19. D	
10. A		20. D	

21. D
22. D
23. D
24. A
25. D

EXAMINATION SECTION
TEST 1

DIRECTIONS: Each question or incomplete statement is followed by several suggested answers or completions. Select the one that BEST answers the question or completes the statement. *PRINT THE LETTER OF THE CORRECT ANSWER IN THE SPACE AT THE RIGHT.*

1. Legal title to a real property passes from seller to buyer when the

    A. deed is delivered
    B. deed is recorded
    C. closing statement is signed
    D. deed is placed in escrow

2. A binder given by a buyer in a real estate transaction

    A. draws interest in favor of the broker
    B. may be withdrawn any time before the seller signs acceptance
    C. must be monetary
    D. must exceed 5 percent of the sales price

3. In a long-term ground lease, the holder of the leased fee is the

    A. grantee   B. grantor   C. lessee   D. lessor

4. A mortgage that covers several parcels of land and contains a provision for partial release upon the sale of a single parcel is called a(n) _____ mortgage.

    A. blanket   B. declining balance
    C. amortized   D. direct reduction

5. When foreclosure expenses and outstanding debts are GREATER than the foreclosure sale proceeds,

    A. the mortgagee must absorb the loss
    B. the mortgagee may obtain a deficiency judgment against the mortgagor
    C. the owner claims statutory right of redemption
    D. there is no solution

6. What is GENERALLY the basis for deciding how much a lender will loan?

    A. List price
    B. Appraised value for loan purposes
    C. Final sales price
    D. Lower value of either the sales price or the appraised value for loan purposes

7. The _____ clause defines or limits the quantity of the estate being conveyed.

    A. reversion   B. partition
    C. revocation   D. habendum

8. Which of the following documents is considered evidence that personal property has been pledged to secure a loan?

   A. Partial release
   B. Bill of sale
   C. Chattel mortgage
   D. Bargain and sale deed

9. A deed may be prepared by a(n)

   A. licensed appraiser
   B. licensed salesperson
   C. attorney or owner of the property
   D. principal broker only

10. If a buyer purchases a furnished fee simple home and is assuming the existing mortgage, the settlement company will have drawn up each of the following EXCEPT the

    A. assumption agreement
    B. note and mortgage
    C. warranty deed
    D. bill of sale

11. A(n) _____ is an easement to the holder of the dominant tenement.

    A. license
    B. encumbrance
    C. appurtenance
    D. encroachment

12. Which of the following has the right to sign the name of a principal to a contract of sale? A(n)

    A. broker with a listing
    B. special agent
    C. attorney-in-fact
    D. attorney-at-law

13. The BEST determination of the difference between police power and eminent domain is whether

    A. owner's use was affected
    B. improvements are to be razed
    C. any compensation was paid to the owner
    D. the action was by sovereign power or statute

14. The document which serves as the BEST evidence of a good title to a property is the

    A. warranty deed
    B. abstract
    C. mortgage
    D. bill of sale

15. Which of the following is NOT considered a valid expense for a building manager to include in a budget?

    A. Cleaning and maintenance supplies
    B. Foundation repairs
    C. Management fees
    D. Heating fuel

16. _____ interest CANNOT be practiced by one who owns a life estate.

    A. Sale of
    B. Devising
    C. Leasing
    D. Mortgage of

17. Which of the following is NOT a function of the Federal National Mortgage Association (FNMA)?

    A. Purchasing conventional loans
    B. Originating federal loans
    C. Buying FHA-DVA loans
    D. Selling mortgages to institutions

18. The word *fee*, in connection with real property, means

    A. an estate of inheritance
    B. the leased land
    C. the money charged by a broker for services
    D. the charge made for searching title

19. A standard form policy of title insurance protects against loss caused by each of the following EXCEPT

    A. liens and encumbrances of record
    B. forgery in the chain of title
    C. encroachment on the property
    D. lack of capacity of the grantor

20. Buying real property *subject to mortgage* is

    A. a type of conditional loan
    B. the right to foreclose without going to court
    C. a mortgage bought by the FNMA and sold to the GNMA
    D. the taking of title by a grantee with no liability for paying the mortgage loan

21. A claim of title by a stranger places which of the following parties in the WEAKEST position?

    A. One who holds an unrecorded deed
    B. One who holds a recorded quitclaim deed to the property
    C. A nonoccupant holder of a warranty deed
    D. A nonoccupant holder of an unrecorded quitclaim deed

22. One of the functions of the recording system is

    A. giving constructive notice of documents
    B. curing major defects in title
    C. insuring title against loss due to third-party claims
    D. handling the closing of real estate transactions

23. In the event of a foreclosure of the subject property, which of the following liens would have TOP priority?

    A. First recorded state income tax lien
    B. Second recorded federal estate tax lien
    C. Mechanic's lien for work begun before any other lien was recorded
    D. Last recorded state property tax lien

24. What is another term for the buyer, or person to whom real estate is conveyed?

   A. Assignee B. Grantee C. Offeror D. Optionee

25. If a lessee defaults on a lease and abandons the property in good condition, he/she could be held liable for the

   A. balance of the rent plus the security deposit
   B. balance of the rent plus the cost of finding a new tenant
   C. balance of the rent
   D. decrease in market value of the property

KEY (CORRECT ANSWERS)

1. A
2. B
3. D
4. A
5. B

6. C
7. D
8. C
9. C
10. B

11. C
12. C
13. C
14. B
15. B

16. B
17. B
18. A
19. C
20. D

21. D
22. A
23. D
24. B
25. C

TEST 2

DIRECTIONS: Each question or incomplete statement is followed by several suggested answers or completions. Select the one that BEST answers the question or completes the statement. *PRINT THE LETTER OF THE CORRECT ANSWER IN THE SPACE AT THE RIGHT.*

1. A principal could NOT establish or maintain a fiduciary relationship with a(n) 1.____
    A. trustee
    B. appraiser
    C. administrator
    D. receiver

2. Which of the following relationships MOST resembles the relationship between a real estate agent and a principal? 2.____
    A. Trustee/beneficiary
    B. Vendee/vendor
    C. Mortgagee/mortgagor
    D. Optionee/optionor

3. The gross income multiplier is calculated by dividing the sales price by the _____ income. 3.____
    A. monthly net
    B. annual gross
    C. monthly gross
    D. annual net

4. A deed that is made and delivered but not recorded is 4.____
    A. valid between the parties and valid as to subsequent recorded interests
    B. valid between the parties and invalid as to subsequent donees of the property
    C. valid between the parties and valid as to third parties with notice
    D. invalid between the parties

5. When a condominium apartment owner defaults in paying state real property taxes, an exercisable option of the taxing agency is to 5.____
    A. force forfeiture of a band from the owner
    B. place a lien on common elements
    C. seek to foreclose against the apartment
    D. seek to recover from the condominium association

6. Which of the following terms MOST closely describes physical deterioration? 6.____
    A. Wear and tear
    B. Reversion
    C. Obsolescence
    D. Recapture

7. If the reproduction cost shows a HIGHER dollar amount than the appraised value, _____ has MOST likely occurred. 7.____
    A. economic obsolescence
    B. excessive appraisal
    C. capitalization
    D. accrued depreciation

8. Which of the following could be considered a variance? A(n) 8.____
    A. old grocery store in an area recently rezoned residential
    B. single-family home in a residential zone
    C. large, new department store located in an area zoned for small retail shops
    D. home much larger and more expensive than adjacent homes

9. Which of the following is NOT generally considered the duty of a property manager?

   A. Investing profits from client properties
   B. Marketing space
   C. Collecting rents
   D. Making minor repairs

10. A real estate salesperson could LEGALLY accept extra commission as compensation for a difficult sale from a

   A. broker-employer
   B. buyer
   C. seller
   D. mortgage lender

11. The recording of a warranty deed

   A. guarantees title
   B. constitutes constructive notice of ownership
   C. verifies title
   D. insures ownership

12. The party to a real estate transaction who is MOST exposed to liability would be the

   A. grantor selling subject to loan
   B. grantee taking subject to loan
   C. grantor in a loan assumption
   D. grantor of a quitclaim deed

13. Which of the following is TRUE of the preparation of a mortgage document?

   A. The seller assumes no financial risk.
   B. A mortgage is required.
   C. The title is conveyed immediately to the buyer.
   D. The seller is the lender.

14. The process that will revert real property to the government when a person dies intestate and no heirs can be found for succession is

   A. reversion
   B. escheat
   C. reconveyance
   D. succession

15. Which of the following is NOT a common purpose for escrow or a settlement agent?

   A. Preparation of legal and tax documents
   B. Assurance of the payment of purchase price
   C. Determination of the satisfaction of outstanding liens
   D. Handling the closing and signing of documents

16. Which of the following is NOT an example of external obsolescence?

   A. Population density
   B. Zoning
   C. Direct effect of elements
   D. Special assessments

17. If an option to purchase is exercised,

    A. the notice to exercise must be in writing
    B. closing occurs on the date the option is exercised
    C. the optionor can be forced to sell the property
    D. the option money is automatically applied to the purchase price

18. When a seller takes back a mortgage from the buyer as part payment for the sale,

    A. the seller retains legal title
    B. the seller is entitled to the property until the debt is paid
    C. this is considered a purchase money mortgage
    D. no second mortgage may be placed on the property by the buyer

19. A purchase money mortgage and a land contract are SIMILAR in that

    A. the seller is the lender
    B. the seller assumes no financial risk
    C. a mortgage is required
    D. title is conveyed immediately to the buyer

20. Which of the following statements is TRUE of deeds?

    A. Bargain and sale deed is illegal.
    B. General warranty deed gives the least liability to the grantor.
    C. Special warranty deed gives the greatest protection to the grantor.
    D. Quitclaim deed gives the least protection to the grantee.

21. A deed that is not dated, recorded, or acknowledged is considered _____ in terms of its validity between grantor and grantee.

    A. invalid   B. void
    C. valid   D. revocable by the grantor

22. Which of the following is considered to possess riparian rights? A(n)

    A. corporation
    B. business trust
    C. owner living in a townhouse subdivision
    D. owner living on a waterway

23. When using the market comparison approach, an appraiser should consider

    A. property tax rates
    B. acquisition cost to present owner
    C. sales price of comparable properties
    D. tax benefits

24. Of the following, only _____ does NOT appear in a promissory note.

    A. interest
    B. purchase price of property
    C. term of loan
    D. commencement date

25. Under a contract of sale in which the date of occupancy is LATER than the settlement date, the

    A. buyer cannot obtain hazard insurance
    B. seller is the legal owner until occupancy has ended
    C. contract should stipulate whether the seller is to pay any rent
    D. buyer does not acquire legal title upon settlement

KEY (CORRECT ANSWERS)

1.	B	11.	B
2.	A	12.	A
3.	B	13.	B
4.	C	14.	B
5.	C	15.	A
6.	A	16.	C
7.	D	17.	C
8.	C	18.	C
9.	A	19.	A
10.	A	20.	D

21. C
22. D
23. C
24. B
25. C

EXAMINATION SECTION
TEST 1

DIRECTIONS: Each question or incomplete statement is followed by several suggested answers or completions. Select the one that BEST answers the question or completes the statement. *PRINT THE LETTER OF THE CORRECT ANSWER IN THE SPACE AT THE RIGHT.*

1. Legal title to a real property passes from seller to buyer when the

    A. deed is delivered
    B. deed is recorded
    C. closing statement is signed
    D. deed is placed in escrow

2. A binder given by a buyer in a real estate transaction

    A. draws interest in favor of the broker
    B. may be withdrawn any time before the seller signs acceptance
    C. must be monetary
    D. must exceed 5 percent of the sales price

3. In a long-term ground lease, the holder of the leased fee is the

    A. grantee   B. grantor   C. lessee   D. lessor

4. A mortgage that covers several parcels of land and contains a provision for partial release upon the sale of a single parcel is called a(n) _____ mortgage.

    A. blanket
    B. declining balance
    C. amortized
    D. direct reduction

5. When foreclosure expenses and outstanding debts are GREATER than the foreclosure sale proceeds,

    A. the mortgagee must absorb the loss
    B. the mortgagee may obtain a deficiency judgment against the mortgagor
    C. the owner claims statutory right of redemption
    D. there is no solution

6. What is GENERALLY the basis for deciding how much a lender will loan?

    A. List price
    B. Appraised value for loan purposes
    C. Final sales price
    D. Lower value of either the sales price or the appraised value for loan purposes

7. The _____ clause defines or limits the quantity of the estate being conveyed.

    A. reversion
    B. partition
    C. revocation
    D. habendum

39

8. Which of the following documents is considered evidence that personal property has been pledged to secure a loan? 8.____

   A. Partial release
   B. Bill of sale
   C. Chattel mortgage
   D. Bargain and sale deed

9. A deed may be prepared by a(n) 9.____

   A. licensed appraiser
   B. licensed salesperson
   C. attorney or owner of the property
   D. principal broker only

10. If a buyer purchases a furnished fee simple home and is assuming the existing mortgage, the settlement company will have drawn up each of the following EXCEPT the 10.____

    A. assumption agreement
    B. note and mortgage
    C. warranty deed
    D. bill of sale

11. A(n) _____ is an easement to the holder of the dominant tenement. 11.____

    A. license
    B. encumbrance
    C. appurtenance
    D. encroachment

12. Which of the following has the right to sign the name of a principal to a contract of sale? A(n) 12.____

    A. broker with a listing
    B. special agent
    C. attorney-in-fact
    D. attorney-at-law

13. The BEST determination of the difference between police power and eminent domain is whether 13.____

    A. owner's use was affected
    B. improvements are to be razed
    C. any compensation was paid to the owner
    D. the action was by sovereign power or statute

14. The document which serves as the BEST evidence of a good title to a property is the 14.____

    A. warranty deed
    B. abstract
    C. mortgage
    D. bill of sale

15. Which of the following is NOT considered a valid expense for a building manager to include in a budget? 15.____

    A. Cleaning and maintenance supplies
    B. Foundation repairs
    C. Management fees
    D. Heating fuel

16. _____ interest CANNOT be practiced by one who owns a life estate. 16.____

    A. Sale of
    B. Devising
    C. Leasing
    D. Mortgage of

17. Which of the following is NOT a function of the Federal National Mortgage Association (FNMA)?

    A. Purchasing conventional loans
    B. Originating federal loans
    C. Buying FHA-DVA loans
    D. Selling mortgages to institutions

18. The word *fee*, in connection with real property, means

    A. an estate of inheritance
    B. the leased land
    C. the money charged by a broker for services
    D. the charge made for searching title

19. A standard form policy of title insurance protects against loss caused by each of the following EXCEPT

    A. liens and encumbrances of record
    B. forgery in the chain of title
    C. encroachment on the property
    D. lack of capacity of the grantor

20. Buying real property *subject to mortgage* is

    A. a type of conditional loan
    B. the right to foreclose without going to court
    C. a mortgage bought by the FNMA and sold to the GNMA
    D. the taking of title by a grantee with no liability for paying the mortgage loan

21. A claim of title by a stranger places which of the following parties in the WEAKEST position?

    A. One who holds an unrecorded deed
    B. One who holds a recorded quitclaim deed to the property
    C. A nonoccupant holder of a warranty deed
    D. A nonoccupant holder of an unrecorded quitclaim deed

22. One of the functions of the recording system is

    A. giving constructive notice of documents
    B. curing major defects in title
    C. insuring title against loss due to third-party claims
    D. handling the closing of real estate transactions

23. In the event of a foreclosure of the subject property, which of the following liens would have TOP priority?

    A. First recorded state income tax lien
    B. Second recorded federal estate tax lien
    C. Mechanic's lien for work begun before any other lien was recorded
    D. Last recorded state property tax lien

24. What is another term for the buyer, or person to whom real estate is conveyed?

    A. Assignee   B. Grantee   C. Offeror   D. Optionee

25. If a lessee defaults on a lease and abandons the property in good condition, he/she could be held liable for the

    A. balance of the rent plus the security deposit
    B. balance of the rent plus the cost of finding a new tenant
    C. balance of the rent
    D. decrease in market value of the property

KEY (CORRECT ANSWERS)

1. A
2. B
3. D
4. A
5. B

6. C
7. D
8. C
9. C
10. B

11. C
12. C
13. C
14. B
15. B

16. B
17. B
18. A
19. C
20. D

21. D
22. A
23. D
24. B
25. C

TEST 2

DIRECTIONS: Each question or incomplete statement is followed by several suggested answers or completions. Select the one that BEST answers the question or completes the statement. *PRINT THE LETTER OF THE CORRECT ANSWER IN THE SPACE AT THE RIGHT.*

1. A principal could NOT establish or maintain a fiduciary relationship with a(n) 1._____

    A. trustee
    B. appraiser
    C. administrator
    D. receiver

2. Which of the following relationships MOST resembles the relationship between a real estate agent and a principal? 2._____

    A. Trustee/beneficiary
    B. Vendee/vendor
    C. Mortgagee/mortgagor
    D. Optionee/optionor

3. The gross income multiplier is calculated by dividing the sales price by the _____ income. 3._____

    A. monthly net
    B. annual gross
    C. monthly gross
    D. annual net

4. A deed that is made and delivered but not recorded is 4._____

    A. valid between the parties and valid as to subsequent recorded interests
    B. valid between the parties and invalid as to subsequent donees of the property
    C. valid between the parties and valid as to third parties with notice
    D. invalid between the parties

5. When a condominium apartment owner defaults in paying state real property taxes, an exercisable option of the taxing agency is to 5._____

    A. force forfeiture of a band from the owner
    B. place a lien on common elements
    C. seek to foreclose against the apartment
    D. seek to recover from the condominium association

6. Which of the following terms MOST closely describes physical deterioration? 6._____

    A. Wear and tear
    B. Reversion
    C. Obsolescence
    D. Recapture

7. If the reproduction cost shows a HIGHER dollar amount than the appraised value, _____ has MOST likely occurred. 7._____

    A. economic obsolescence
    B. excessive appraisal
    C. capitalization
    D. accrued depreciation

8. Which of the following could be considered a variance? A(n) 8._____

    A. old grocery store in an area recently rezoned residential
    B. single-family home in a residential zone
    C. large, new department store located in an area zoned for small retail shops
    D. home much larger and more expensive than adjacent homes

43

9. Which of the following is NOT generally considered the duty of a property manager?

    A. Investing profits from client properties
    B. Marketing space
    C. Collecting rents
    D. Making minor repairs

10. A real estate salesperson could LEGALLY accept extra commission as compensation for a difficult sale from a

    A. broker-employer
    B. buyer
    C. seller
    D. mortgage lender

11. The recording of a warranty deed

    A. guarantees title
    B. constitutes constructive notice of ownership
    C. verifies title
    D. insures ownership

12. The party to a real estate transaction who is MOST exposed to liability would be the

    A. grantor selling subject to loan
    B. grantee taking subject to loan
    C. grantor in a loan assumption
    D. grantor of a quitclaim deed

13. Which of the following is TRUE of the preparation of a mortgage document?

    A. The seller assumes no financial risk.
    B. A mortgage is required.
    C. The title is conveyed immediately to the buyer.
    D. The seller is the lender.

14. The process that will revert real property to the government when a person dies intestate and no heirs can be found for succession is

    A. reversion
    B. escheat
    C. reconveyance
    D. succession

15. Which of the following is NOT a common purpose for escrow or a settlement agent?

    A. Preparation of legal and tax documents
    B. Assurance of the payment of purchase price
    C. Determination of the satisfaction of outstanding liens
    D. Handling the closing and signing of documents

16. Which of the following is NOT an example of external obsolescence?

    A. Population density
    B. Zoning
    C. Direct effect of elements
    D. Special assessments

17. If an option to purchase is exercised,

    A. the notice to exercise must be in writing
    B. closing occurs on the date the option is exercised
    C. the optionor can be forced to sell the property
    D. the option money is automatically applied to the purchase price

18. When a seller takes back a mortgage from the buyer as part payment for the sale,

    A. the seller retains legal title
    B. the seller is entitled to the property until the debt is paid
    C. this is considered a purchase money mortgage
    D. no second mortgage may be placed on the property by the buyer

19. A purchase money mortgage and a land contract are SIMILAR in that

    A. the seller is the lender
    B. the seller assumes no financial risk
    C. a mortgage is required
    D. title is conveyed immediately to the buyer

20. Which of the following statements is TRUE of deeds?

    A. Bargain and sale deed is illegal.
    B. General warranty deed gives the least liability to the grantor.
    C. Special warranty deed gives the greatest protection to the grantor.
    D. Quitclaim deed gives the least protection to the grantee.

21. A deed that is not dated, recorded, or acknowledged is considered _____ in terms of its validity between grantor and grantee.

    A. invalid   B. void
    C. valid   D. revocable by the grantor

22. Which of the following is considered to possess riparian rights? A(n)

    A. corporation
    B. business trust
    C. owner living in a townhouse subdivision
    D. owner living on a waterway

23. When using the market comparison approach, an appraiser should consider

    A. property tax rates
    B. acquisition cost to present owner
    C. sales price of comparable properties
    D. tax benefits

24. Of the following, only _____ does NOT appear in a promissory note.

    A. interest
    B. purchase price of property
    C. term of loan
    D. commencement date

25. Under a contract of sale in which the date of occupancy is LATER than the settlement date, the

   A. buyer cannot obtain hazard insurance
   B. seller is the legal owner until occupancy has ended
   C. contract should stipulate whether the seller is to pay any rent
   D. buyer does not acquire legal title upon settlement

KEY (CORRECT ANSWERS)

1. B
2. A
3. B
4. C
5. C

6. A
7. D
8. C
9. A
10. A

11. B
12. A
13. B
14. B
15. A

16. C
17. C
18. C
19. A
20. D

21. C
22. D
23. C
24. B
25. C

EXAMINATION SECTION
TEST 1

DIRECTIONS: Each question or incomplete statement is followed by several suggested answers or completions. Select the one that BEST answers the question or completes the statement. *PRINT THE LETTER OF THE CORRECT ANSWER IN THE SPACE AT THE RIGHT.*

1. Legal title to a real property passes from seller to buyer when the

    A. deed is delivered
    B. deed is recorded
    C. closing statement is signed
    D. deed is placed in escrow

    1.____

2. A binder given by a buyer in a real estate transaction

    A. draws interest in favor of the broker
    B. may be withdrawn any time before the seller signs acceptance
    C. must be monetary
    D. must exceed 5 percent of the sales price

    2.____

3. In a long-term ground lease, the holder of the leased fee is the

    A. grantee   B. grantor   C. lessee   D. lessor

    3.____

4. A mortgage that covers several parcels of land and contains a provision for partial release upon the sale of a single parcel is called a(n) _____ mortgage.

    A. blanket
    C. amortized
    B. declining balance
    D. direct reduction

    4.____

5. When foreclosure expenses and outstanding debts are GREATER than the foreclosure sale proceeds,

    A. the mortgagee must absorb the loss
    B. the mortgagee may obtain a deficiency judgment against the mortgagor
    C. the owner claims statutory right of redemption
    D. there is no solution

    5.____

6. What is GENERALLY the basis for deciding how much a lender will loan?

    A. List price
    B. Appraised value for loan purposes
    C. Final sales price
    D. Lower value of either the sales price or the appraised value for loan purposes

    6.____

7. The _____ clause defines or limits the quantity of the estate being conveyed.

    A. reversion
    C. revocation
    B. partition
    D. habendum

    7.____

47

8. Which of the following documents is considered evidence that personal property has been pledged to secure a loan?

   A. Partial release
   B. Bill of sale
   C. Chattel mortgage
   D. Bargain and sale deed

9. A deed may be prepared by a(n)

   A. licensed appraiser
   B. licensed salesperson
   C. attorney or owner of the property
   D. principal broker only

10. If a buyer purchases a furnished fee simple home and is assuming the existing mortgage, the settlement company will have drawn up each of the following EXCEPT the

    A. assumption agreement
    B. note and mortgage
    C. warranty deed
    D. bill of sale

11. A(n) _____ is an easement to the holder of the dominant tenement.

    A. license
    B. encumbrance
    C. appurtenance
    D. encroachment

12. Which of the following has the right to sign the name of a principal to a contract of sale? A(n)

    A. broker with a listing
    B. special agent
    C. attorney-in-fact
    D. attorney-at-law

13. The BEST determination of the difference between police power and eminent domain is whether

    A. owner's use was affected
    B. improvements are to be razed
    C. any compensation was paid to the owner
    D. the action was by sovereign power or statute

14. The document which serves as the BEST evidence of a good title to a property is the

    A. warranty deed
    B. abstract
    C. mortgage
    D. bill of sale

15. Which of the following is NOT considered a valid expense for a building manager to include in a budget?

    A. Cleaning and maintenance supplies
    B. Foundation repairs
    C. Management fees
    D. Heating fuel

16. _____ interest CANNOT be practiced by one who owns a life estate.

    A. Sale of
    B. Devising
    C. Leasing
    D. Mortgage of

17. Which of the following is NOT a function of the Federal National Mortgage Association (FNMA)?

    A. Purchasing conventional loans
    B. Originating federal loans
    C. Buying FHA-DVA loans
    D. Selling mortgages to institutions

18. The word *fee*, in connection with real property, means

    A. an estate of inheritance
    B. the leased land
    C. the money charged by a broker for services
    D. the charge made for searching title

19. A standard form policy of title insurance protects against loss caused by each of the following EXCEPT

    A. liens and encumbrances of record
    B. forgery in the chain of title
    C. encroachment on the property
    D. lack of capacity of the grantor

20. Buying real property *subject to mortgage* is

    A. a type of conditional loan
    B. the right to foreclose without going to court
    C. a mortgage bought by the FNMA and sold to the GNMA
    D. the taking of title by a grantee with no liability for paying the mortgage loan

21. A claim of title by a stranger places which of the following parties in the WEAKEST position?

    A. One who holds an unrecorded deed
    B. One who holds a recorded quitclaim deed to the property
    C. A nonoccupant holder of a warranty deed
    D. A nonoccupant holder of an unrecorded quitclaim deed

22. One of the functions of the recording system is

    A. giving constructive notice of documents
    B. curing major defects in title
    C. insuring title against loss due to third-party claims
    D. handling the closing of real estate transactions

23. In the event of a foreclosure of the subject property, which of the following liens would have TOP priority?

    A. First recorded state income tax lien
    B. Second recorded federal estate tax lien
    C. Mechanic's lien for work begun before any other lien was recorded
    D. Last recorded state property tax lien

24. What is another term for the buyer, or person to whom real estate is conveyed? 24.____

    A. Assignee   B. Grantee   C. Offeror   D. Optionee

25. If a lessee defaults on a lease and abandons the property in good condition, he/she could be held liable for the 25.____

    A. balance of the rent plus the security deposit
    B. balance of the rent plus the cost of finding a new tenant
    C. balance of the rent
    D. decrease in market value of the property

KEY (CORRECT ANSWERS)

1. A
2. B
3. D
4. A
5. B
6. C
7. D
8. C
9. C
10. B
11. C
12. C
13. C
14. B
15. B
16. B
17. B
18. A
19. C
20. D
21. D
22. A
23. D
24. B
25. C

TEST 2

DIRECTIONS: Each question or incomplete statement is followed by several suggested answers or completions. Select the one that BEST answers the question or completes the statement. *PRINT THE LETTER OF THE CORRECT ANSWER IN THE SPACE AT THE RIGHT.*

1. A principal could NOT establish or maintain a fiduciary relationship with a(n) 1.____
    - A. trustee
    - B. appraiser
    - C. administrator
    - D. receiver

2. Which of the following relationships MOST resembles the relationship between a real estate agent and a principal? 2.____
    - A. Trustee/beneficiary
    - B. Vendee/vendor
    - C. Mortgagee/mortgagor
    - D. Optionee/optionor

3. The gross income multiplier is calculated by dividing the sales price by the _____ income. 3.____
    - A. monthly net
    - B. annual gross
    - C. monthly gross
    - D. annual net

4. A deed that is made and delivered but not recorded is 4.____
    - A. valid between the parties and valid as to subsequent recorded interests
    - B. valid between the parties and invalid as to subsequent donees of the property
    - C. valid between the parties and valid as to third parties with notice
    - D. invalid between the parties

5. When a condominium apartment owner defaults in paying state real property taxes, an exercisable option of the taxing agency is to 5.____
    - A. force forfeiture of a band from the owner
    - B. place a lien on common elements
    - C. seek to foreclose against the apartment
    - D. seek to recover from the condominium association

6. Which of the following terms MOST closely describes physical deterioration? 6.____
    - A. Wear and tear
    - B. Reversion
    - C. Obsolescence
    - D. Recapture

7. If the reproduction cost shows a HIGHER dollar amount than the appraised value, _____ has MOST likely occurred. 7.____
    - A. economic obsolescence
    - B. excessive appraisal
    - C. capitalization
    - D. accrued depreciation

8. Which of the following could be considered a variance? A(n) 8.____
    - A. old grocery store in an area recently rezoned residential
    - B. single-family home in a residential zone
    - C. large, new department store located in an area zoned for small retail shops
    - D. home much larger and more expensive than adjacent homes

9. Which of the following is NOT generally considered the duty of a property manager?

   A. Investing profits from client properties
   B. Marketing space
   C. Collecting rents
   D. Making minor repairs

10. A real estate salesperson could LEGALLY accept extra commission as compensation for a difficult sale from a

    A. broker-employer   B. buyer
    C. seller   D. mortgage lender

11. The recording of a warranty deed

    A. guarantees title
    B. constitutes constructive notice of ownership
    C. verifies title
    D. insures ownership

12. The party to a real estate transaction who is MOST exposed to liability would be the

    A. grantor selling subject to loan
    B. grantee taking subject to loan
    C. grantor in a loan assumption
    D. grantor of a quitclaim deed

13. Which of the following is TRUE of the preparation of a mortgage document?

    A. The seller assumes no financial risk.
    B. A mortgage is required.
    C. The title is conveyed immediately to the buyer.
    D. The seller is the lender.

14. The process that will revert real property to the government when a person dies intestate and no heirs can be found for succession is

    A. reversion   B. escheat
    C. reconveyance   D. succession

15. Which of the following is NOT a common purpose for escrow or a settlement agent?

    A. Preparation of legal and tax documents
    B. Assurance of the payment of purchase price
    C. Determination of the satisfaction of outstanding liens
    D. Handling the closing and signing of documents

16. Which of the following is NOT an example of external obsolescence?

    A. Population density
    B. Zoning
    C. Direct effect of elements
    D. Special assessments

17. If an option to purchase is exercised,

    A. the notice to exercise must be in writing
    B. closing occurs on the date the option is exercised
    C. the optionor can be forced to sell the property
    D. the option money is automatically applied to the purchase price

18. When a seller takes back a mortgage from the buyer as part payment for the sale,

    A. the seller retains legal title
    B. the seller is entitled to the property until the debt is paid
    C. this is considered a purchase money mortgage
    D. no second mortgage may be placed on the property by the buyer

19. A purchase money mortgage and a land contract are SIMILAR in that

    A. the seller is the lender
    B. the seller assumes no financial risk
    C. a mortgage is required
    D. title is conveyed immediately to the buyer

20. Which of the following statements is TRUE of deeds?

    A. Bargain and sale deed is illegal.
    B. General warranty deed gives the least liability to the grantor.
    C. Special warranty deed gives the greatest protection to the grantor.
    D. Quitclaim deed gives the least protection to the grantee.

21. A deed that is not dated, recorded, or acknowledged is considered _____ in terms of its validity between grantor and grantee.

    A. invalid
    B. void
    C. valid
    D. revocable by the grantor

22. Which of the following is considered to possess riparian rights? A(n)

    A. corporation
    B. business trust
    C. owner living in a townhouse subdivision
    D. owner living on a waterway

23. When using the market comparison approach, an appraiser should consider

    A. property tax rates
    B. acquisition cost to present owner
    C. sales price of comparable properties
    D. tax benefits

24. Of the following, only _____ does NOT appear in a promissory note.

    A. interest
    B. purchase price of property
    C. term of loan
    D. commencement date

25. Under a contract of sale in which the date of occupancy is LATER than the settlement date, the

    A. buyer cannot obtain hazard insurance
    B. seller is the legal owner until occupancy has ended
    C. contract should stipulate whether the seller is to pay any rent
    D. buyer does not acquire legal title upon settlement

KEY (CORRECT ANSWERS)

1.	B	11.	B
2.	A	12.	A
3.	B	13.	B
4.	C	14.	B
5.	C	15.	A
6.	A	16.	C
7.	D	17.	C
8.	C	18.	C
9.	A	19.	A
10.	A	20.	D

21. C
22. D
23. C
24. B
25. C

EXAMINATION SECTION
TEST 1

DIRECTIONS: Each question or incomplete statement is followed by several suggested answers or completions. Select the one that BEST answers the question or completes the statement. *PRINT THE LETTER OF THE CORRECT ANSWER IN THE SPACE AT THE RIGHT.*

1. The title to land held in absolute ownership is

   A. a leasehold
   B. record title
   C. fee simple
   D. ownership in common

2. The first instrument a buyer usually signs in a real estate transaction is a

   A. mortgage
   B. deed
   C. bill of sale
   D. offer to purchase

3. The interest on $7,500 for 4 months at 5 1/2% per annum is

   A. $75.50   B. $250.10   C. $137.50   D. $195.60

4. In order to accurately ascertain the correct boundaries of real property, one should obtain a(n)

   A. title policy
   B. bill of sale
   C. survey
   D. abstract

5. The person who conveys title to real estate is called the

   A. grantee   B. devision   C. trustee   D. grantor

6. A written agreement giving the agent a right to collect a commission, no matter who sells the property, is an

   A. option
   B. open listing
   C. exclusive right to sell
   D. open lease

7. The state of ownership of real property where the undivided interest of two or more owners is with survivorship is known as estate

   A. by the entirety
   B. by surety right
   C. in joint tenancy
   D. in common

8. When a person has an interest in land which is to continue as long as he lives, he is said to have a(n)

   A. estate for years
   B. easement
   C. option for years
   D. life estate

9. An absolute, basic requirement of a simple contract is

   A. witnesses
   B. acknowledgment by a notary public
   C. an official recording
   D. offer and acceptance

10. An option without a valid consideration is

    A. valid
    B. unforceable
    C. void
    D. binding

11. The tax on a given piece of property is determined by multiplying the tax rate by the

    A. selling price
    B. value of the property
    C. insured value
    D. assessed valuation of the property

12. The landlord is called

    A. legatee   B. devisee   C. lessor   D. mortgagor

13. In the sale of mortgaged property, it is necessary

    A. to obtain the consent of the mortgagee
    B. to pay off the mortgage
    C. for the grantor to deliver the deed
    D. to obtain a court order

14. An option contract differs from a contract of sale in that the

    A. option need not be consummated
    B. option needs no consideration
    C. contract of sale is enforceable on either party to in
    D. contract of sale requires consideration

15. To *alienate* property, one

    A. advertises it for sale
    B. sells it to a foreigner
    C. conveys title
    D. uses it for payment of judgment in a suit of alienation of affections

16. To foreclose a mortgage without power of sale, one must

    A. go to Court
    B. secure a release
    C. discharge the indebtedness
    D. execute a reconveyance deed

17. A guarantee that title to real property is as represented is called a

    A. warranty
    B. certificate of title
    C. condition precedent
    D. title search

18. A licensed real estate salesman is permitted by law to represent

    A. several brokers
    B. only his employing broker
    C. himself as broker
    D. an interested third party

19. A mortgage is a person who

   A. borrows money and puts up his property as security
   B. lends money to a mortgagor
   C. leases real property for a consideration
   D. purchases real property on the installment plan

20. The legal rights which a wife possesses upon the death of her husband in lands owned by him in fee simple is called

   A. courtesy B. legal share
   C. share by entirety D. dower

21. A contract which provides for the payment of a commission to a broker, even though the owner makes the sale without the aid of the broker, is called

   A. exclusive listing B. open listing
   C. exclusive right to sell D. option

22. If you purchase a property and want the fullest security with your deed, which instrument would you use? _____ deed.

   A. Quit claim B. Special warranty
   C. Warranty D. Grant

23. Where do you file your deed of record? At the

   A. title company B. state land department
   C. county clerk D. county recorder's office

24. You record a deed for which reason or reasons?
   I. Make it valid
   II. For safety
   III. Gives notice to the world
   IV. Insures certain title
   V. Required by the state
   VI. Clear off any indebtedness
   VII. Save title insurance cost

   The CORRECT combination is:

   A. I, III, V, VII B. III, IV, VI
   C. I, II, III D. II, III

25. To which documents is the transfer tax applied?
   I. Release of mortgage
   II. Quit claim deed
   III. Contract of sale
   IV. Special warranty deed
   V. Bill of sale
   VI. Easement
   VII. Warranty deed
   VIII. Grant deed

   The CORRECT combination is:

   A. I, II, IV, VIII B. II, III, VII
   C. IV, V, VI, VII D. IV, VII, VIII

KEY (CORRECT ANSWERS)

1. C
2. D
3. C
4. C
5. D

6. C
7. C
8. D
9. D
10. C

11. D
12. C
13. C
14. A
15. C

16. A
17. B
18. B
19. B
20. D

21. C
22. C
23. D
24. D
25. D

TEST 2

DIRECTIONS: Each question or incomplete statement is followed by several suggested answers or completions. Select the one that BEST answers the question or completes the statement. *PRINT THE LETTER OF THE CORRECT ANSWER IN THE SPACE AT THE RIGHT.*

1. A real estate salesman is paid by the

    A. seller
    B. buyer
    C. broker to whom his license is issued
    D. escrow agent

    1.____

2. A real estate salesman is entitled to receive

    A. one half of the 5% commission
    B. what the broker decides is fair
    C. what he has earned according to his agreement with the broker
    D. all of the above

    2.____

3. A listing is

    A. an option
    B. a land contract
    C. property for sale
    D. the broker's contract of employment with an owner to find a purchaser for the owner's property

    3.____

4. Every real estate license must be registered at the

    A. office of real estate commission
    B. local real estate board
    C. county clerk's office
    D. recorder's office

    4.____

5. The deposit of a buyer is given

    A. as part payment of the purchase price
    B. to cover escrow expenses
    C. to assure the broker and salesman of a commission
    D. to be forfeited if the deal fails

    5.____

6. A deed to convey marketable title must be signed by the

    A. seller and his wife
    B. grantors and grantees
    C. sellers, buyers, and broker
    D. mortgagors and mortgages

    6.____

7. Legal title to real estate passes when

    A. a duly executed deed is delivered to the buyer
    B. the deed is properly signed
    C. the deed is notarized and sealed
    D. the deed is recorded

    7.____

59

8. The license of a real estate broker or salesman may be revoked or suspended for violation of the real estate license law by the

   A. division of licenses and permits
   B. court of common pleas
   C. National Association of Real Estate Boards
   D. real estate commission

8.____

9. When a salesman is discharged or leaves the employ of a broker, the broker should

   A. give the salesman his license
   B. notify the local real estate board
   C. inform the salesman by telephone
   D. send salesman's license to the state real estate commission

9.____

10. Title to real estate is conveyed when the

    A. act of sale is recorded
    B. act of sale is signed by parties
    C. copy of act of sale is received
    D. parties agree to sell to buyer

10.____

11. To operate a branch office, a broker must

    A. find a good location
    B. have his license endorsed to cover branch office
    C. obtain a branch office license from the state real estate commission
    D. have 10 years' experience

11.____

12. All listings shall be taken in the name of the

    A. buyer
    B. seller
    C. salesman (licensed)
    D. principal licensed broker

12.____

13. In order to ascertain the exact boundaries of a property, you should obtain

    A. a copy of the title
    B. an abstract of title
    C. statements of adjoining owners
    D. a survey by a registered surveyor

13.____

14. A real estate salesman, upon receiving a deposit, should

    A. turn it over to seller, less commission
    B. use it to cover expenses of transaction
    C. give it to broker to be placed in an escrow account
    D. give party for the office staff

14.____

15. A fundamental requirement of a contract is 15._____

    A. offer and acceptance
    B. acknowledgment by a notary public
    C. recordation at court house
    D. use of the proper printed form

16. A copy of a broker's bond should be 16._____

    A. kept in a bank box
    B. displayed in the broker's office in public view
    C. kept in the office safe
    D. carried on the broker's person

17. Upon being sued in a real estate transaction, a salesman or broker should 17._____

    A. notify the state real estate commission
    B. leave the state
    C. effect a compromise
    D. declare bankruptcy

18. A salesman's license stays in the possession of 18._____

    A. the salesman   B. the commission
    C. his broker   D. his next of kin

19. A percentage lease is usually based on a percentage of the 19._____

    A. assessed value of the property
    B. gross sales of the business
    C. tenant's net worth
    D. market value of the property

20. Anyone operating in the real estate brokerage business without a license 20._____

    A. is subject to a fine or imprisonment, or both
    B. is considered unethical
    C. is barred from ever getting a license
    D. cannot hire a licensed salesman

21. A broker should furnish a bond 21._____

    A. in the required amount
    B. in the parish of his residence
    C. after he has been sued
    D. if he is insolvent

22. When a broker and salesman have a dispute over commission, they should 22._____

    A. discuss it with buyer and seller
    B. consult their attorneys
    C. contact the commission in writing
    D. request a hearing from the commission

23. The amount of commission to be paid a broker is fixed by 23.____

    A. statute law
    B. the lending bank
    C. the real estate commission
    D. agreement of the parties

24. If an owner refuses to pay a commission, a broker should 24.____

    A. request a salesman to deal with the party
    B. turn the matter over to an attorney
    C. complain to the purchaser
    D. tear up all agreements

25. In taking an inventory of a place of business, one should 25.____

    A. exclude all items under $1.00
    B. be as fast as possible
    C. number each article with chalk
    D. write contents down in detail, have parties initial each page, and sign last page

---

KEY (CORRECT ANSWERS)

1.	C	11.	C
2.	C	12.	D
3.	D	13.	D
4.	C	14.	C
5.	A	15.	A
6.	A	16.	B
7.	A	17.	A
8.	D	18.	C
9.	D	19.	B
10.	B	20.	A

21.	A
22.	B
23.	D
24.	B
25.	D

EXAMINATION SECTION
TEST 1

DIRECTIONS: Each question consists of a statement. You are to indicate whether the statement is TRUE (T) or FALSE (F). PRINT THE LETTER OF THE CORRECT ANSWER IN THE SPACE AT THE RIGHT.

1. Power of attorney can be given only to duly qualified attorneys at law. 1.____

2. If the broker holds an exclusive listing, he is entitled to his commission even if the owner himself sells the property before the expiration date of such listing. 2.____

3. A deed to be valid requires the signatures of both the grantor and grantee. 3.____

4. The term *appraised value* means the present market value. 4.____

5. The real estate commission is empowered to subpoena persons to produce books and papers at a formal hearing for the revocation of a license. 5.____

6. A broker should consent to the transfer of a salesman's license even though the salesman owes him money which the broker loaned him. 6.____

7. The mortgagor is the party who loans the money. 7.____

8. A salesman may advertise in his own name without mentioning his broker. 8.____

9. A broker can collect his commission on an oral listing of real estate if given in the presence of witnesses. 9.____

10. The committing of one act prohibited by the real estate license law constitutes a violation. 10.____

11. Permanent buildings on real estate are not personal property. 11.____

12. Title to real estate is passed by delivery of the abstract. 12.____

13. The term *assessed valuation* always means market price. 13.____

14. The sale of a property for cash automatically cancels an eight-month lease. 14.____

15. Objectionable features which materially reduce the value of property should be called to the prospect's attention before taking a deposit. 15.____

16. An alien may not be licensed as a salesman even though he received his first papers. 16.____

17. A real estate salesman may be associated with a limited real estate broker. 17.____

18. A real estate broker can deposit his license with the commission and obtain a real estate saleman's license. 18.____

19. A real estate salesman can deposit his license with the real estate commission. 19.____

20. An address change application, a fee and the broker's license must be submitted to the office at once upon an address change as opposed to making the change at renewal time on the continuation authority. 20.____

21. A real estate salesman can collect in his own name money in connection with a real estate transaction.   21._____

22. It is a violation of the real estate license law for a real estate broker or real estate salesman to offer as an inducement to enter into a contract for the purchase or sale of real estate anything of value other than the consideration recited in the sales contract.   22._____

23. A real estate broker must notify the commission in writing immediately upon receipt of notice from the surety that the surety has made payment on the broker's bond.   23._____

24. A real estate broker should keep his license in a safety deposit vault or other safe place so that it cannot be lost or stolen.   24._____

25. *Exclusive Listing* is the same as *Exclusive Right* to sell.   25._____

KEY (CORRECT ANSWERS)

1.	F		11.	T
2.	F		12.	F
3.	F		13.	F
4.	F		14.	F
5.	T		15.	T
6.	T		16.	T
7.	F		17.	F
8.	F		18.	T
9.	T		19.	F
10.	T		20.	T

21. F
22. T
23. T
24. F
25. F

TEST 2

DIRECTIONS: Each question consists of a statement. You are to indicate whether the statement is TRUE (T) or FALSE (F). *PRINT THE LETTER OF THE CORRECT ANSWER IN THE SPACE AT THE RIGHT.*

1. A broker may sell his own personal property to a client without disclosing that fact.   1.____

2. The amount of money to be deposited with an *Offer to Buy* is fixed by law.   2.____

3. A quit claim deed may convey fee title to real estate.   3.____

4. A city lot 49' x 187' contains 8163 square feet of land.   4.____

5. As soon as his license is received from the real estate commission, the new real estate broker is entitled to use the word *Realtor* on signs, stationery, and advertising.   5.____

6. Zoning laws are local regulations to beautify cities.   6.____

7. An applicant for salesman's license must be a citizen of the United States.   7.____

8. Restrictions are limitations upon the use of property by deed or law.   8.____

9. The rights of a party in possession need not be considered in negotiating the sale of real property.   9.____

10. Complete and accurate records of real estate transactions need not be kept by the broker if the deal is satisfactorily closed.   10.____

11. The salesman should open a separate account for the deposits he receives.   11.____

12. The terms *option* and *listing* have the same meaning.   12.____

13. Open listing means the price is not set.   13.____

14. A salesman must include name of his broker in his advertisements.   14.____

15. The December payment of taxes generally covers the last half of the year.   15.____

16. It is necessary that a licensed real estate broker erect a sign where he has his office, on which shall be plainly stated that he is a licensed real estate broker.   16.____

17. Either the salesman or the broker must witness the contract.   17.____

18. Grantees should always witness the deed.   18.____

19. A salesman may split a commission with any other licensed salesman or broker.   19.____

20. The commission may, on its own motion, investigate any action of a licensee and call the matter for a hearing.   20.____

21. The commission may revoke a broker's license as well as a salesman's license if the salesman is found guilty of conduct of fraudulent or dishonest dealing.   21.____

22. A friend of a broker, not in any way connected with the real estate business, may receive a bonus or a gift, as long as it is not a stated or computed commission, for assisting in making a deal. 22.____

23. The house number and street address is sufficient description to set out the property to be conveyed by a quit claim deed. 23.____

24. A first mortgage is always a first lien. 24.____

25. It is NOT important to specify the amount of commission to be charged for the sale of real estate because that is fixed by law. 25.____

KEY (CORRECT ANSWERS)

1. F
2. F
3. T
4. F
5. F

6. F
7. T
8. T
9. F
10. F

11. F
12. F
13. F
14. T
15. F

16. T
17. F
18. F
19. F
20. T

21. T
22. F
23. F
24. F
25. F

TEST 3

DIRECTIONS: Each question consists of a statement. You are to indicate whether the statement is TRUE (T) or FALSE (F). *PRINT THE LETTER OF THE CORRECT ANSWER IN THE SPACE AT THE RIGHT.*

1. If two parties to an escrow make conflicting demands upon the escrow holder, he may refuse to act further until an agreement has been reached or until the courts have directed the disposition of the instruments and the money deposited in the escrow. 1.____

2. A broker must immediately notify the commission when he changes his business address. 2.____

3. An owner of a business lot sold it at a figure approximately twice its cost. In showing the adjoining lot to a prospective buyer, a real estate broker is entirely within his rights to make a definite promise of a similar profit to his customer. 3.____

4. A salesman may NOT sue anyone except his broker for the collection of a real estate commission. 4.____

5. A licensed salesman may divide his commission with another licensed salesman with a broker's consent. 5.____

6. A person who sells a property under an order of court is not required to have a license. 6.____

7. Assessments are for the support of the Government. 7.____

8. A male minor of 20 years can acquire but cannot convey real estate in most states. 8.____

9. Escrow is another name for a husband's interest in his wife's property. 9.____

10. Building restrictions as shown in a deed are NOT encumbrances. 10.____

11. Trees, shrubs, and vines are real property while in the ground. 11.____

12. The commission may refuse to issue, revoke, or suspend a license immediately upon receiving a serious complaint against a broker or salesman. 12.____

13. A broker who knows that misrepresentations are being made by his salesmen may have his license revoked, even though he, himself, is not guilty of making the misrepresentation. 13.____

14. A broker accepting a net listing to sell a piece of real property should NOT accept any compensation from the purchaser unless he reveals this fact to the seller. 14.____

15. It is NOT necessary for a person to hold a real estate license to execute, buy, or sell an option. 15.____

16. A real estate broker or salesman should keep his license in a safety box or other safe place so that it cannot be lost or stolen. 16.____

17. *Exclusive Listing* is the same as *Exclusive or Sole Right* to sell. 17.____

18. A *Good* and *Valuable* consideration is the same. 18.____

19. Procedure for revocation provides for immediate revocation of a license on filing of complaint. 19.____

20. Employees in the office of real estate broker who are strictly clerical need NOT be licensed. 20.____

21. If a prospective purchaser revokes his offer in writing before he has received an accepted copy of the offer to purchase, signed by the seller, he is entitled to the return of his deposit. 21.____

22. Real estate listings may be taken in the name of the salesman so long as any deal is closed in the name of the employing broker. 22.____

23. When a property is sold on which an easement exists, it should be shown in the conveyance. 23.____

24. An owner should NEVER be given a copy of the listing form he signs. 24.____

25. Taxes have priority over recorded mortgages. 25.____

KEY (CORRECT ANSWERS)

1.	T	11.	T
2.	T	12.	F
3.	F	13.	T
4.	T	14.	T
5.	F	15.	F
6.	T	16.	F
7.	F	17.	F
8.	T	18.	F
9.	F	19.	F
10.	F	20.	T

21. T
22. F
23. T
24. F
25. T

TEST 4

DIRECTIONS: Each question consists of a statement. You are to indicate whether the statement is TRUE (T) or FALSE (F). *PRINT THE LETTER OF THE CORRECT ANSWER IN THE SPACE AT THE RIGHT.*

1. A person who was licensed in 2000 upon application, may secure a license for the current year without taking an examination. 1.____

2. It is lawful for a salesman to complete a deal, collect commission in his own name, and then give his broker his agreed share. 2.____

3. Legal descriptions of property are NOT required in a lease. 3.____

4. A broker is required to notify the commission immediately after a salesman leaves his employ. 4.____

5. It is NOT a violation of law for a broker to pay a commission directly to a salesman employed by another broker. 5.____

6. The death of an owner terminates any listing given by him. 6.____

7. The commission has ruled that 5% is the standard commission to be charged on the sale of city property. 7.____

8. If only the wife signs a listing on a home, in the event that the broker sells it, he could not bring suit against the husband and secure a judgment for his commission. 8.____

9. Only attorneys at law may hold a valid power of attorney. 9.____

10. Rezoning residence lots into business lots always increases their value. 10.____

11. A *certificate of title* indemnifies the holder against the loss sustained due to errors made in searching the records. 11.____

12. A *guarantee of title* and a *policy of title insurance* give the same protection to the property owner. 12.____

13. Taxes become liens against real property on January 1st. 13.____

14. An option for which no consideration is given is NOT enforceable. 14.____

15. A lease is a contract. 15.____

16. A recorded mortgage has priority over a street assessment made against a property at a later date. 16.____

17. A listing contract is terminated by the death of the principal. 17.____

18. The real estate commission may revoke a broker's or a salesman's license if the salesman is found guilty of conduct of fraudulent or dishonest dealing. 18.____

19. A salesman must maintain a sign to indicate he is a licensed salesman-- his name must be clearly shown. 19.____

20. Officer-of-corporation license does not authorize the holder to act other than as the company's designated representative. 20._____

21. A friend of a broker, not in any way connected with the real estate business, may receive a bonus or gift, as long as it is not a stated or computed commission, for assisting in making a deal. 21._____

22. A broker or salesman who violated a provision of the real estate license law two years ago is still subject to penalty for such violation. 22._____

23. A person last licensed as a broker or salesman in 1975 may, upon application, secure a license for the current year without taking an examination. 23._____

24. Legal descriptions of property are NOT required in a lease. 24._____

25. If your neighborhood merchant (who has no real estate license) assists you in the sale of a $100,000 lot, on which you receive a brokerage commission of 5%, you may lawfully give him 1/2 of same for his help in the transaction. 25._____

KEY (CORRECT ANSWERS)

1.	F	11.	F
2.	F	12.	F
3.	T	13.	T
4.	T	14.	T
5.	F	15.	T
6.	T	16.	F
7.	F	17.	T
8.	T	18.	T
9.	F	19.	F
10.	F	20.	T

21.	F
22.	T
23.	F
24.	T
25.	F

TEST 5

DIRECTIONS: Each question consists of a statement. You are to indicate whether the statement is TRUE (T) or FALSE (F). *PRINT THE LETTER OF THE CORRECT ANSWER IN THE SPACE AT THE RIGHT.*

1. A broker must be the procuring cause to be entitled to a commission on an open listing. 1.____

2. An exclusive listing cannot be terminated. 2.____

3. Deeds and mortgages are recorded in the country clerk's office, in the county where the lands are situated. 3.____

4. A mechanic's lien is an encumbrance. 4.____

5. Revocation of the broker's license automatically suspends the salesman's license. 5.____

6. An open listing is more advantageous to a broker than an exclusive listing. 6.____

7. The filing of an application for a license allows the applicant to operate. 7.____

8. A bill of sale can be substituted for a deed in the transfer of real estate. 8.____

9. If you, a salesman for Broker A, with your Broker's consent, make a deal with Broker B, he, Broker B, knowing you are licensed, can pay you your earned portion of the commission. 9.____

10. As soon as the grantor signs the deed and has the same acknowledged, title passes to the grantee. 10.____

11. The earnest money receipt is one of the most important, if not the most important, instruments in a real estate transaction. 11.____

12. An estate is an interest which one has in property. 12.____

13. A written contract holds over a verbal contract. 13.____

14. The market value of a home is the cost of the lot, plus the present-day replacement cost of the building thereon. 14.____

15. One real transaction requires a license. 15.____

16. If a broker thinks there will be future profits from the resale of the property he is selling, he may so guarantee them to his client. 16.____

17. Personal property may become real property when it is permanently attached to the deed. 17.____

18. A mortgage is a conveyance. 18.____

19. An attachment is a voluntary lien. 19.____

20. An ordinary lease is personal property and is a personal estate. 20.____

21. As soon as his license is received from the real estate commission, the new real estate broker is entitled to use the word REALTOR on signs, stationery, and advertising.   21._____

22. Engaging in real estate business without a license constitutes a misdemeanor.   22._____

23. A broker is not required to give the real estate commission notice if he moves his office to another location in the same community.   23._____

24. A broker who collects rents for clients and commingles the money with his own so that he cannot make proper accounting, may have his license revoked.   24._____

25. Re-zoning residence lots into business lots always increases the value of the residence lots.   25._____

KEY (CORRECT ANSWERS)

1. T
2. F
3. F
4. T
5. T

6. F
7. F
8. F
9. F
10. F

11. T
12. T
13. T
14. F
15. T

16. F
17. T
18. T
19. F
20. T

21. F
22. T
23. F
24. T
25. F

TEST 6

DIRECTIONS: Each question consists of a statement. You are to indicate whether the statement is TRUE (T) or FALSE (F). *PRINT THE LETTER OF THE CORRECT ANSWER IN THE SPACE AT THE RIGHT.*

1. A licensed salesman may go to work for another broker immediately upon the filing of a request for transfer.   1.____
2. The *Statute of Frauds* requires all contracts to be in writing.   2.____
3. Most State constitutions prohibit aliens from owning land in the United States.   3.____
4. Each branch office of a broker must be in the charge of a licensed broker or salesman.   4.____
5. All listings secured by a salesman belong to the broker.   5.____
6. A real estate salesman should carry his license at all times to properly identify himself.   6.____
7. *Specific performance* is a court action to compel performance of a contract.   7.____
8. The commission has the power to subpoena records in real estate transactions.   8.____
9. Failure to give the buyer a copy of the offer he signs is reason for the rejection of a real estate license.   9.____
10. A real estate salesman must turn all deposits over to his broker.   10.____
11. An abstract is a history of title to real property.   11.____
12. Title insurance offers protection against loss by fire.   12.____
13. A survey is a measurement of land by a qualified surveyor.   13.____
14. A lien is a charge against property for a debt.   14.____
15. The term, Encumbrance, includes any legal claim against property.   15.____
16. An employee who only solicits listings need not be licensed.   16.____
17. A mortgage is given as security for a debt.   17.____
18. An easement is a license to go on another's land.   18.____
19. A contract is an agreement expressed or implied to do or not to do a certain thing.   19.____
20. Another name for a note is mortgage.   20.____
21. The real estate license law was instituted in your state SOLELY to secure revenue for the State.   21.____
22. Only the mortgagor's signature is acknowledged on a mortgage.   22.____
23. A broker is NOT permitted to ratify an unauthorized act executed by one of his salesmen.   23.____

24. Loss is on the buyer if the contract makes no reference to fire loss risk prior to the closing. 24._____

25. After a lease has been assigned, the assignor is no longer liable for the rent. 25._____

KEY (CORRECT ANSWERS)

1. F
2. F
3. F
4. T
5. T

6. F
7. T
8. T
9. T
10. T

11. T
12. F
13. T
14. T
15. T

16. F
17. T
18. T
19. T
20. F

21. F
22. T
23. F
24. F
25. F

EXAMINATION SECTION
TEST 1

DIRECTIONS: Each question consists of a statement. You are to indicate whether the statement is TRUE (T) or FALSE (F). *PRINT THE LETTER OF THE CORRECT ANSWER IN THE SPACE AT THE RIGHT.*

1. The *laws of selling* work just as well for any type of real estate transaction. 1.____

2. The saying that *a good appraiser makes a poor salesman* and the statement that a good salesman becomes a better salesman by increasing his knowledge of appraisal, have equal validity. 2.____

3. Since there are differences in quantity and quality of facilities provided by a real estate office, the basic necessities of adequate listings, available prospects, and cooperative atmosphere are not USUALLY found in all. 3.____

4. There is little difference between wanting to earn a commission and wanting to make a sale. 4.____

5. A penetrating study of the buyer's needs, motivations, and abilities are necessary details for the successful salesman. 5.____

6. Seventy-five percent of salesmen sell only 20% of the property while 25% sell 80% of the property. 6.____

7. Real estate is a percentage business. 7.____

8. The fewer calls–the more listings–the more prospects–the more closings–and the more earnings. 8.____

9. You must compete with your fellow real estate brokers and salesmen to see that this year is better than last, and that the next will beat this one. 9.____

10. The routine procedures such as listing, showing, closing, leasing, trading, floor duty, and services for people, do NOT constitute selling. 10.____

11. Seventy-five percent of the sale is *the approach*. 11.____

12. Of the five senses of seeing, hearing, feeling, tasting, or smelling, sight, e.g., a picture of the property, is much the MOST important. 12.____

13. While no one wants to be sold, psychologically people want to buy. 13.____

14. A built-in sales resistance keeps people *buyers* and not *shoppers*. 14.____

15. People have a sales resistance because of limited funds, fear of being pushed into a decision, and countless other reasons. 15.____

16. Everything in selling is affected by the law of averages. The less you do, the more you achieve. 16.____

17. It is a selling gospel that if you ask enough people to buy real estate, you will have a handsome income. The salesmen who listen to this advice and follow it are very successful. 17.____

18. You need other people listing and selling to maintain market activity. 18.____

19. Home buyers act because of emotional motives, while the investor is prompted by rational motives. 19.____

20. Because people want a sound structure, they do not buy amenities such as comfort, convenience, security, and pleasure. 20.____

21. Memorized discussions based on the motives of *profit and savings, pride and prestige,* and *safety and security of family* can be used with success. 21.____

22. Every listed property MUST be inspected inside and outside. 22.____

23. An over-priced listing is a saleable item. 23.____

24. If an owner tells you that another property in the neighborhood sold for a certain figure, and you know this information is in error, it is IMPROPER to tell him what his neighbor really got. 24.____

25. The neighborhood of a newly listed property is a very fertile source of good prospects. 25.____

KEY (CORRECT ANSWERS)

1.	T	11.	T
2.	T	12.	T
3.	F	13.	T
4.	F	14.	F
5.	T	15.	T
6.	T	16.	F
7.	T	17.	T
8.	F	18.	T
9.	F	19.	T
10.	F	20.	F

21. T
22. T
23. F
24. F
25. T

TEST 2

DIRECTIONS: Each question consists of a statement. You are to indicate whether the statement is TRUE (T) or FALSE (F). *PRINT THE LETTER OF THE CORRECT ANSWER IN THE SPACE AT THE RIGHT.*

1. If your knowledge of the neighborhood has shown you that there are no young children, do sell the property to the parents of an only child. 1.____

2. People who seek to purchase real estate MUST respond to a great many personal questions if they are to be helped. It is up to the broker or salesman to overcome the natural resentment people have for others prying into their affairs. 2.____

3. In this connection, a check list clipped to an Earnest Money form has little advantage. 3.____

4. Tell the owner to stay away from you during the showing. 4.____

5. If possible, have the husband and wife together during the showing. 5.____

6. If only one is present at the showing and the unusual happens, such as *it's just what we want,* have that individual sign the Earnest Money Receipt there and then. 6.____

7. Every property has its best side. That is the side you should approach. 7.____

8. In showing the property, refrain from pointing out an obvious disadvantage or the need for any improvements that should be made. 8.____

9. Every successful salesman agrees that one should never argue with a customer. 9.____

10. Many salesmen and many brokers come back from a showing so badly shaken and SOLD by the prospect that they can talk of nothing but the things wrong with the property. Know your merchandise and this cannot happen to you. 10.____

11. The objections to the purchase of a real property that fills the wants and fits the needs of a prospect are rather standard. 11.____

12. When you are quoting a price to a potential buyer, spell it out, *nine thousand four hundred dollars.* When you tell the seller of the offer, put it in the short form, *ninety-four hundred dollars.* 12.____

13. There is a set formula for closing the sale—a single demonstration. 13.____

14. The task is NOT *how* to close but *when* to close. 14.____

15. Since it is human nature to fear signing something that obligates you to make future payments, all salesmen anticipates fear of the Earnest Money Receipt by keeping it carefully concealed during the showing. 15.____

16. Few salesmen believe in the trial close, or multiple closing technique. 16.____

17. Multiple closing requires close attention to every word and mannerism of the prospect. 17.____

18. Alertness to the moods of your prospect and suggested actions for him to take, represent *high pressure* selling, even if used with good sense. 18.____

19. The BEST way for a real estate salesman to sell a house is by not *selling* it. 19._____

20. The key to the sale of a home is to prove to the prospective buyer that the value of the home will be worth more than the money paid for it. 20._____

21. The personality of a real estate salesman is NOT so important a factor as it is in the selling of a less vital and expensive product. 21._____

22. The easiest of all canvassing jobs is the search for properties to sell. 22._____

23. The canvassing salesman who asks the question several times a day, *Have you ever thought of selling your house?,* finds it helps to use *home* when talking to an owner and *house* when talking with a potential buyer. 23._____

24. A poor question for the canvassing salesman to ask occupants who are renting is, *Have you ever thought of the money you would make by owning your own home?* 24._____

25. When the owner asks you, *What should I ask for this house?,* you should come up with a fast answer before he changes his mind. 25._____

KEY (CORRECT ANSWERS)

1.	F	11.	T
2.	T	12.	F
3.	F	13.	F
4.	T	14.	T
5.	T	15.	F
6.	T	16.	F
7.	T	17.	T
8.	F	18.	F
9.	T	19.	T
10.	T	20.	T

21. T
22. F
23. F
24. F
25. F

EXAMINATION SECTION
TEST 1

DIRECTIONS: Each question consists of a statement. You are to indicate whether the statement is TRUE (T) or FALSE (F). *PRINT THE LETTER OF THE CORRECT ANSWER IN THE SPACE AT THE RIGHT.*

1. In most real estate transactions in which he is involved, the real estate broker acts as an agent for someone else the principal—who seeks to sell to or to buy from or exchange real property or a business opportunity with a third party.   1.____

2. It is NOT important to distinguish agency from other types of relationships.   2.____

3. Numerous complaints come to the attention of State real estate authorities resulting from the efforts of licensees to secure large profits from the transactions they handle by attempting to act on their own accounts or, in effect, as principals.   3.____

4. The use of options and net listings is illegal or unethical even in those cases where a full disclosure of the broker's status and the legal effect on the paper signed is made to the persons with whom he is dealing.   4.____

5. A broker normally would be classified as an employee.   5.____

6. The CHIEF consideration which determines one to be an independent contractor is the fact that the employer has the right of control as to the mode or method of doing the work contracted for.   6.____

7. An independent contractor may, nevertheless, be an agent; the real estate broker is USUALLY in this category.   7.____

8. The situation in which the distinction between employee and independent contractor become most important are in the fields of public liability, workmen's compensation, social security, and unemployment insurance.   8.____

9. Normally, the status of real estate agent is created ONLY by express contract.   9.____

10. Consideration is essential to the creation of an agency.   10.____

11. The first act that takes place between broker and client is the written contract of employment.   11.____

12. The USUAL contract creating the relationship of brokerage merely authorizes the broker to find a purchaser.   12.____

13. Most contracts require the personal performance of the original agent although the latter remains liable for the details delegated to and executed by others.   13.____

14. When the principal executes and entrusts to the agent an instrument negotiable or non-negotiable containing blanks and the agent fills them in, the principal will be bound to third persons who rely upon the instrument, even though the agent was not so authorized.   14.____

15. An agency to sell carries with it the authority to modify or cancel the contract of sale after it has been made. 15.____

16. Generally, an act may be ratified by any words or conduct showing an intention upon the part of the principal to adopt the agent's act as his own. 16.____

17. No liability is incurred by the principal for acts of the agent beyond the scope of his actual or ostensible authority. 17.____

18. When the buyer pays the money into the hands of the broker, the broker holds it as the agent of the buyer and not the seller, and any misappropriation thereof is the loss of the former and not the latter. 18.____

19. If money is paid to the broker upon his agreement to return the same to the buyer upon certain conditions, and such conditions do happen, the broker is liable for the return of the money even though he has paid it to the principal. 19.____

20. One of the LEAST frequent causes of complaint coming to the State real estate authorities arises out of deposits and the demand for their return. 20.____

21. The deposit money NEVER belongs to the broker. 21.____

22. The broker may commingle the principal's money or property with his own. 22.____

23. The fiduciary character with which the broker is clothed throughout the course of his dealings with his client is the LEAST important and outstanding phase of the relationship. 23.____

24. An agent may unite his personal and representative characters in the same transaction. 24.____

25. An agent or employee CAN compete with his principal on matters connected with the agency and, or course, can act as an agent for a competitor. 25.____

KEY (CORRECT ANSWERS)

1. T
2. F
3. T
4. F
5. F

6. F
7. T
8. T
9. T
10. T

11. T
12. T
13. F
14. T
15. F

16. T
17. T
18. T
19. T
20. F

21. T
22. F
23. F
24. F
25. F

TEST 2

DIRECTIONS: Each question consists of a statement. You are to indicate whether the statement is TRUE (T) or FALSE (F). *PRINT THE LETTER OF THE CORRECT ANSWER IN THE SPACE AT THE RIGHT.*

1. The dual agency is a ground for rescission by either principal, without any necessity for showing injury. 1.____

2. A real estate broker when acting as such, in effect, contracts to protect his employer. 2.____

3. The principles of law governing the relation of agent and principal are to the effect that the agent may be allowed to profit at the expense of his principal, no matter whether the result is reached by misrepresentation or concealment or other fraudulent device. 3.____

4. A real estate salesman is NOT subject to the obligation created by a fiduciary relationship since he is an employee of the broker. 4.____

5. A salesman is an employee of the broker, who engages himself to do and is licensed to do ONLY a few of the same things which a broker himself is licensed to do. 5.____

6. Ordinarily, the agent acts with authority for the principal in the name of the principal. 6.____

7. The principal also is bound by his act and only he can sue. 7.____

8. Ordinarily, the agent will be liable on a written contract made in the name of the principal. 8.____

9. In general, when an agent negotiates or paves the way for a contract for his principal with a third party, the contract arises between the principal and the agent. 9.____

10. The real estate broker is generally unlawfully practicing law in filling in the ordinary and usual stereotyped forms used in his business. 10.____

11. Torts are private injuries or wrongs committed upon the victim's person or property, and arising from a breach of duty created by contract rather than by law. 11.____

12. An agent is not liable to third parties for his own torts if the agent acts in accordance with the principal's directions. 12.____

13. The liability of the seller, as principal, for the fraudulent statements of his real estate broker while negotiating a sale is substantially the same as the liability of the employer for the negligence of his employee who runs over a pedestrian while driving the employer's car. 13.____

14. Statements by the broker that his property is the *best on the street* or that the buyer *will receive handsome profits from this investment* normally would be considered merely expressions of opinion and neither civil liability nor liability under the real estate law would be present. 14.____

15. The false representation by a broker of the owner's lowest price acceptable for a piece of property is NOT actionable because it is not a representation of a material fact. 15.____

16. A misstatement of fact, so long as it actually does not affect the value of the property, is NOT actionable. 16.____

17. A material statement made at a time when the speaker knows the statement to be false is clearly fraud. 17.____

18. A broker is NOT really hired or paid by the seller for doing such things as ordering title reports, filling out forms, processing loan applications, ordering pest control reports, and preparing escrow instructions. 18.____

19. Although the agent is always liable for his own torts (civil wrongs), regardless of the liability or nonliability of his principal, the agent is NOT liable for his principal's torts. 19.____

20. No real estate salesman shall be employed by or accept compensation from any person other than the broker under whom he is at the time listed. 20.____

21. In an action for commissions, the plaintiff must allege and prove that he was duly licensed at the time of the transaction in order to recover. 21.____

22. It is unlawful for an licensed real estate salesman to pay any compensation for performing any of the acts within the scope of the regulations to any real estate licensee except through the broker under whom he is at the time licensed. 22.____

23. To be entitled to a commission, the broker must produce *a buyer ready, willing and able to purchase* upon the exact terms and at the price stipulated by the principal. 23.____

24. The real estate broker's most fundamental rights to compensation are based upon his original written employment contract (listing). 24.____

25. The essence of the broker's right to a commission is that it is dependent upon success, and that it, in no way, depends upon, or is affected by, the amount of work done by the broker. 25.____

KEY (CORRECT ANSWERS)

1.	T		11.	F
2.	T		12.	F
3.	F		13.	T
4.	F		14.	T
5.	F		15.	T
6.	T		16.	T
7.	T		17.	T
8.	F		18.	T
9.	F		19.	T
10.	F		20.	T

21. T
22. T
23. T
24. T
25. T

TEST 3

DIRECTIONS: Each question consists of a statement. You are to indicate whether the statement is TRUE (T) or FALSE (F). *PRINT THE LETTER OF THE CORRECT ANSWER IN THE SPACE AT THE RIGHT.*

1. Under brokerage, the broker's or salesman's attention is focused on the legal aspects of real estate, while, under the heading of agency, it is directed to the business aspects. 1.____

2. The fiduciary and trust relationship implicit in the agency relationship permeates real estate brokerage practice. 2.____

3. Selling is the chief purpose in real estate brokerage. 3.____

4. Once you have hurdled the statutory requirement of successfully passing the examination for license as a salesman or broker, your future in real estate is assured. 4.____

5. Selling real estate is different from selling experience in other lines in that the product is LESS complex and individualized and there are standard units. 5.____

6. Selling real estate is different from selling experience in other lines in that the product often represents the largest single purchase the buyer will ever make. 6.____

7. The psychology or predicted behavior of parties involved is LESS complicated in home selling than in selling more personalized consumer goods. 7.____

8. A salesman may get good, indifferent, or no training depending on his selection of the brokerage firm with which he affiliates. 8.____

9. Residential selling probably accounts for more than 75 percent of sales made by the typical realty office. 9.____

10. Insurance is a natural feeder business or extra source of income for the ambitious real estate broker. 10.____

11. A beginning real estate salesman USUALLY must go through an apprenticeship, working for and under the direction of a broker on a commission basis. 11.____

12. USUALLY we find salaried personnel in the real estate business, including the office force in the smaller operations. 12.____

13. Credit plays a small role in the real estate brokerage business. 13.____

14. Selling real estate is USUALLY selling down payment and terms of credit. 14.____

15. Brokers and salesmen need NOT know the source for securing the necessary credit or become involved in expediting loan placement. 15.____

16. In playing the role of a negotiator, the broker can have little influence on the size of the down payment and the balance of payment due the seller. 16.____

17. A broker, in negotiating a loan, SHOULD be guided in his questioning of the applicant by the information which will be required of him by the lender or lenders who will eventually pass upon the loan. 17.____

18. All institutions make FHA or VA loans. 18._____

19. Some institutions will make their own investigation of the moral risk, but few will demand 19._____
    or take into consideration the opinion of the broker.

20. A fundamental understanding of the procedure and instruments used in connection with 20._____
    loans on real estate need be possessed ONLY by the specialist in the real estate office.

21. When a person acts for a compensation in negotiating a new loan, or for selling an exist- 21._____
    ing note secured by real estate, he is required to be licensed as a real estate broker or
    salesman.

22. The term *closing* is often used WITHOUT stating the exact kind of closing that is meant. 22._____
    Actually, there are three meanings of the term *closing*.

23. All listings are the property of the employing broker and NOT of the salesman who may 23._____
    have listed the property.

24. The salesman or broker will be much better off if he will concentrate on *open* listings 24._____
    rather than on exclusive listings.

25. When a lending agency orders a search made, it has the same purpose in mind as the 25._____
    purchaser.

KEY (CORRECT ANSWERS)

1.	F		11.	T
2.	T		12.	F
3.	T		13.	F
4.	F		14.	T
5.	F		15.	F
6.	T		16.	F
7.	F		17.	T
8.	T		18.	F
9.	T		19.	F
10.	T		20.	F

21. T
22. T
23. T
24. F
25. F

EXAMINATION SECTION
TEST 1

DIRECTIONS: In continuous discourse, briefly and concisely answer the following questions.

1. What is the position of the real estate broker with reference to the attorneys of the buyers and seller?

ANSWER
In closing sales and leases, the broker should always recommend the employment of competent legal counsel; many misunderstandings arise out of the doubtless sincere but erroneous advice of these not skilled in the complexities of the law; *home-made* contracts frequently result in trouble and litigation, with a consequent loss to the broker of prestige and good will. The proper fees of the attorneys are paid by the buyer and seller. When the broker fails to recommend legal counsel, he may be injuring not only himself, but those whose interests he is required to protect. A satisfied client is always potentially a *repeat customer* and an asset to any broker.

2. Is it good policy for a broker to give a copy of the listing agreement to the owner who employs him?

ANSWER
The listing form is a contract and each party to the agreement is entitled to a copy. If the broker's employer is furnished with copies of all listings and other agreements, many future misunderstandings will be avoided. The requirement is that the broker or salesman *shall* give the owner a true, legible carbon copy of the listing.

3. May a real estate salesman be lawfully employed by or accept compensation from any broker other than the broker under whom he is licensed at the time?

ANSWER
No. Such employment is prohibited by agency law, which in its broadest sense would seem to make any other employment unlawful, referring directly to the so-called *part time* salesman.

4. Where a real estate salesman employed by one broker is assisted in a transaction by a real estate salesman employed by another broker, under an arrangement whereby both salesmen are to have a part of the commission, is it lawful for the first to pay directly to the second salesman the latter's share of the commission?

ANSWER
No. Payment to the second salesman must be made through his employer broker.

5. Assume that after a listing is taken, and earnest money receipt signed, or a contract executed, a slight change is made in the terms or conditions, and the broker, in the presence of the interested parties, alters the writing to conform to the new arrangement; what precaution should the broker take to protect himself against future misunderstandings?

ANSWER
Always and without exception, he should have all parties to the contract place their signatures or initials in the margin opposite or nearest the alteration. A better practice is to have the document entirely rewritten.

6. What may a licensed real estate broker lawfully do that a licensed real estate salesman may not do lawfully? 6.____

ANSWER
Among other things, a salesman may not transact any phase of the real estate brokerage business in his own name, all must be transacted in the name of the broker by whom he is employed. These phases include: opening and maintaining an office, employing salesmen, listing, advertising, soliciting, negotiating, taking deposits, issuing earnest money receipts, closing transaction, dividing commission, etc.

7. Where a real estate broker who is employed to sell a particular property, buys it himself, but in the name of a *dummy,* will the sale stand if attacked? 7.____

ANSWER
No. As agent for the seller, it is the broker's duty to get as much for the property as possible; as buyer, it is to the broker's interest to acquire the property as cheaply as possible; in such a situation there is a direct conflict between duty and self interest; therefore, it is well established that if a broker desires to purchase the property himself, he must before so doing, advise the owner to the effect, if the owner then is willing to proceed, the sale is valid; if the broker does not make a full disclosure, the sale may be set aside. There is nothing inherently wrong in a broker buying his employer's property; the wrong lies in not advising the employer of the broker's true interest in the matter.

8. A broker is employed by an owner to sell a particular property. He introduces a prospective purchaser to the owner, who, a short time later, cancels the contract of employment. Some time later the owner sells to this prospect. Is the broker entitled to his commission? 8.____

ANSWER
Yes, in all ordinary cases. The law of agency requires the owner to exercise towards the broker the same good faith as is required of the broker in his dealings with his employer.

9. Is a real estate broker liable in law for frauds and misrepresentations of a salesman working out of his office, where the broker had no knowledge of the misrepresentations and did not participate in them? 9.____

ANSWER
Probably yes; if the fraud and misrepresentation were practiced in connection with real estate the broker had for sale.

10. Is a real estate salesman liable to third persons for the misrepresentation of the broker with whom he is associated? 10.____

ANSWER
Not unless he participated therein.

11. Why is it necessary that a contract employing a real estate broker to sell real estate for a commission be in writing? 11.____

ANSWER
The Statute of Frauds provides that unless such contracts, or some sufficient memo thereof, are in writing, signed by the employer, they are void.

12. **How is the Statute of Frauds usually interpreted by the courts?**

    ANSWER

    Strictly against the broker. He has no standing in most courts unless his contract of employment is in writing.

13. **What is the position of a broker, who accepts oral employment to sell real estate, and then finds a purchaser who buys the property and pays the owner his full asking price?**

    ANSWER

    In view of the Statute of Frauds, the broker is helpless to recover compensation, wholly irrespective of the fact that the owner has derived a substantial benefit: the law regards the broker as a mere volunteer, offering and giving his services gratuitously. (See the next question for the proper procedure in a similar situation.) Some states are contra, however.

14. **Assume that a real estate broker is orally employed to sell real estate; he finds a purchaser to whom he gives a receipt for the earnest money; he then secures the owner's written approval of the sale and the latter's written agreement to pay a commission; is the broker then entitled to his commission?**

    ANSWER

    Yes, provided that the papers sufficiently describe the property, name the parties, the amount of the commission, and either authorize or employ the broker named therein to sell the property, or ratify his employment.

15. **What is the difference between a contract giving a broker the exclusive right to sell and a contract giving him an exclusive agency listing with reference to real property?**

    ANSWER

    In a contract for the exclusive right to sell real property, the owner is bound to pay a commission in case of a sale by any person, including himself; while in a contract providing for an exclusive agency listing, the owner merely agrees to employ no other broker in the sale of his property and the owner may sell the property himself without becoming liable for the commission.

TEST 2

DIRECTIONS: In continuous discourse, briefly and concisely answer the following questions.

1. If a husband employs a real estate broker to sell real estate and the broker procures a purchaser ready, able and willing to buy on the husband's exact terms, and the wife then refuses to sign the deed so that the sale is never consummated, is the broker entitled to collect his commission, and if so, from whom?

   1.__

   ANSWER

   Yes. From the husband.

2. If one employs a broker to sell real estate in which he has no interest whatsoever and the broker finds a purchaser ready, willing and able to buy the real estate on the exact terms and for the exact price stated in the listing contract and then the employer, having no title, is unable to convey, is the broker entitled to his commission?

   2.__

   ANSWER

   Yes. The broker has fully performed all that he agreed to do and is entitled to the agreed commission.

3. What compensation can a broker recover for services in bringing about a sale of real estate where his contract of employment does not specify the amount thereof?

   3.__

   ANSWER

   The Statute of Frauds provides in effect that a contract employing a broker to sell real estate must be in writing and if not in writing the contract is void. It occasionally happens that such a contract, though written, fails to specify the amount or rate of compensation to be paid the broker. In some states, the brokerage contract may be enforceable although oral. It is only prudent that, for a broker to recover a commission, for services rendered in connection with the sale of real estate, he should see to it that the amount and the rate of his commission are clearly specified in writing in his contract with his principal; for, if the contract is silent on this point, he may recover nothing, even though his efforts have resulted in the sale of the property, in some states. In other states, however, he can recover the reasonable value of his services. Now, it must be remembered that the final paragraph of an Earnest Money Agreement is a contract between broker and seller, and that extreme care should be used to see that the dollars and cents of commission to be paid is correctly entered.

   In the employment contract, the compensation is shown as a percent of the selling price. In the earnest money agreement the percentage (actual amount) is shown. Do not get carried away and change the 6% of the employment contract to the decimal .06 in the earnest money – you might get just that – 6 cents.

4. Under what circumstances may a broker receive compensation from both parties to the same transaction? Can a broker represent both the seller and purchaser in a sale or exchange of real estate and collect a commission from both?

   4.__

   ANSWER

   This question has been discussed by the courts upon several occasions and the circumstances outlined under which the broker's double employment is allowable. The rule is that if one employs a broker or accepts his services with knowledge of his employment by another, the written agreement to pay commission can be enforced, if the transaction is otherwise fair and honorable.

The reason for the foregoing rule is based upon the fact that one cannot exercise his whole duty to two principals whose interests are conflicting, it being the duty of the agent for the seller to sell for the highest price and the duty of the agent for the buyer to buy for the lowest price.

5. Where a real estate broker having no written contract for a commission brings about an exchange of properties and the parties to the exchange in their agreement with each other agree to pay a commission, may the broker recover the same?

5.____

ANSWER

No. The law governing the collection of real estate broker's commission requires that every commission contract be in writing, and provides that if the same is not in writing the contract is void and the commission is not collectible. In construing the Statute of Frauds, the courts have repeatedly held that it does not matter how efficient the broker may have been in bringing about a sale or how meritorious the services of the broker may have been, if the agreement to pay a commission is not embodied in writing, signed by the party to be charged, which shows the contracting parties, intelligently identifies the property involved, discloses the terms and conditions of the agreement, and expresses a consideration, the broker is helpless, legally, to collect the promised commission, notwithstanding that he brought about a sale accepted by the owner.

6. Where an owner of real estate authorizes a broker to sell his property at a certain price, and the broker finds a purchaser who pays to the broker a deposit of earnest money to bind the sale, and the owner then refuses to convey, who is liable to the purchaser for the return of the earnest money, the broker or the owner?

6.____

ANSWER

In most of the cases where this question is involved, the broker is found trying to retain the earnest money on the theory that it is due him from the owner as a commission. Though recognizing that the broker has a valid claim against the owner, courts everywhere hold that the broker must look directly to the owner for his compensation, and that he cannot retain the deposit, thus, in effect, forcing the purchaser to pay the owner's debts.

7. What is a sufficient description of real estate in a contract to buy or exchange the same? Must a correct legal description be given, or is it sufficient to refer to the land in general terms?

7.____

ANSWER

A writing concerned with the sale of real property must identify the latter. It is common to say that the writing must describe the property, but the connotation of the word *describe* exacts more than the Statute of Frauds requires. Parol evidence may be used for the purpose of supplying the description to the land, but it is never a valid substitute for missing description. – *In the present instance, no part of the writing gives any indication whatever of the city, county or state in which the property is located; nor does it mention the place where the agreement was effected or the parties reside. As already indicated, no one with the paper in his hand would have any idea where to go in search of the property. In short, a material part of the description is missing and no part of the writing points to the source of evidence aliunde which will identify the property.*

8. Is it correct practice for a salesman to complete a sale and collect in his own name the commission and then give his broker-employer his share of the commission?

8.____

ANSWER
No. The salesman has no right to collect the commission; that right belongs exclusively to his employer; should the salesman receive the commission, he should deliver it immediately to his employer.

9. When earnest money is received by a salesman, is he at liberty to make use of it for his personal account up to the amount of his share of the commission before the deal is closed? If not, what should he do with it?

ANSWER
No. Deposits of earnest money should be delivered by the salesman to his employer immediately; there are no exceptions to this rule.

10. Is it legal for a broker to place a sign on property without the consent of the owner?

ANSWER
No.

11. If a broker is assisted by his grocer in procuring a prospect or in closing a deal, is it lawful for the broker to pay the grocer for his services a fair and reasonable portion of his commission?

ANSWER
No.

12. Is it lawful for a broker to agree with a tenant of the house which the broker has for sale to pay the tenant a portion of the commission should a prospect to whom the tenant shows the property later buy the same?

ANSWER
No.

13. Is it lawful for a broker to pay any third person a stated sum for services rendered in connection with showing the property or assisting in a real estate transaction?

ANSWER
No. Such a payment can not be made whether contingent or otherwise.

14. May a broker's or salesman's license be removed for guaranteeing or promising to a prospective purchaser a definite quick profit on the resale of the property?

ANSWER
No.

15. Does the real estate commissioner have power to compel a broker or salesman to make restitution in cases of fraud and misrepresentation?

ANSWER
No. His sole power is to suspend or revoke licenses.

16. What is meant by *consideration?*

ANSWER
Without being too technical, *consideration* when used with reference to a real estate contract is synonymous with the word *inducement.* Consideration is *that which induces a*

person to act or promise. It is *some benefit or advantage to the party promising.* Consideration may be money, property, the performance of services or anything else which the law recognizes as having a value.

17. If a broker receives more than one bona fide offer for the same property at approximately the same date, should he select the one to be submitted to the owner?

    ### ANSWER
    No. All bona fide offers, as soon as received, should be submitted to the owner. It is for the owner to determine which offer, if any, should be accepted. The broker should not exercise any discretion in the matter.

18. What is the effect of a deed conveying real estate to husband and wife?

    ### ANSWER
    A deed conveying real estate to a husband and wife creates what is legally known as an *estate by the entireties,* the chief feature of which is the *Tight of survivorship.* If one spouse dies, the surviving spouse takes the whole property free from all claims of the heirs and creditors of the deceased spouse. There is neither dower nor curtesy as to real estate held in the names of husband and wife, as such, agree to purchase real estate will create an estate by the entireties in the properties to be purchased.

19. Where real estate is conveyed to a husband and wife, thus creating an estate by the entireties, and the husband dies, what problem' or other proceedings are necessary before the surviving wife lawfully may sell and convey the prooerty?

    ### ANSWER
    Absolutely none.

20. In a contract for the sale of real estate, John Smith is the purchaser or vendee. He sells his interest to a third person and desires to assign the contract. Is it necessary for his wife to join the assignment?

    ### ANSWER
    Yes, in order to bar a possible dower right.

EXAMINATION SECTION
TEST 1

DIRECTIONS: Each question consists of a statement. You are to indicate whether the statement is TRUE (T) or FALSE (F). *PRINT THE LETTER OF THE CORRECT ANSWER IN THE SPACE AT THE RIGHT.*

1. A contract is an exchange of promises or assents by two or more persons, for the breach of which the law gives a remedy, or the performance of which the law in some way recognizes as a duty. 1.____

2. A contract can be expressed or implied. 2.____

3. A contract may be oral. 3.____

4. A unilateral contract is made if a promise of one party is given in exchange for the promise of another party. 4.____

5. A bilateral contract is made if one party promises something to induce the other to act, such as the promise to pay a reward for recovery of a lost dog. 5.____

6. A contract is executed when both parties have fully performed under a contract. 6.____

7. A contract is voidable when something remains to be done by either party. 7.____

8. A contract is binding and enforceable against both parties is valid. 8.____

9. A voidable contract is simply a non-existent contract. 9.____

10. A void contract is one binding and enforceable on its face, but one in which one party USUALLY has an option to void or validate as he chooses, and subject to certain conditions. 10.____

11. In real estate, the MOST usual voidable contracts are in transactions involving a minor. 11.____

12. Most states require a broker to be 21 years of age because until he is 21 years old he is NOT legally competent to enter into a contract. 12.____

13. It is important in any contract that there be a *meeting of the minds*. There MUST be actual offer and acceptance with all parties furnishing legal consideration. 13.____

14. Misrepresentation, if proven, is grounds for recission of a contract. 14.____

15. The Listing Agreement and Employment Contract is the contract employing a broker to buy or sell real estate for compensation or commission. 15.____

16. The Earnest Money Receipt or Agreement is the contract for the sale of real property or an interest therein. 16.____

17. The Earnest Money Receipt is a contract between three parties. 17.____

18. An agreement for the sale of real property is outside the Statute of Frauds. 18.____

19. An agreement for the sale of real property MUST be in writing only if it is not to be performed within one year. 19._____

20. A contract need ONLY be signed by one party to be valid. 20._____

21. If the commission percentage to the broker is left out of the employment contract, the court will fill in the USUAL amount of percentage paid to brokers. 21._____

22. Everyone interested in a contract of sale of real property MUST be designated with all possible certainty so that all parties having an interest in the fee will be bound by the contract and any decree for specific performance will affect all persons required to execute a deed sufficient to convey marketable title. 22._____

23. Specific performance under a contract refers to an order of the court to do specifically what a party to a contract promised to do. 23._____

24. A spouse has a dower or curtesy right in the property as long as the marital relationship continues. 24._____

25. If the spouse has NOT joined in the contract of sale as one of the sellers there is no way whatsoever that the buyer can require this spouse to join in the ultimate deed to the property. 25._____

KEY (CORRECT ANSWERS)

1.	T	11.	T
2.	T	12.	T
3.	T	13.	T
4.	F	14.	T
5.	F	15.	T
6.	T	16.	T
7.	F	17.	T
8.	T	18.	F
9.	F	19.	F
10.	F	20.	F

21.	F
22.	T
23.	T
24.	T
25.	T

TEST 2

DIRECTIONS: Each question consists of a statement. You are to indicate whether the statement is TRUE (T) or FALSE (F). *PRINT THE LETTER OF THE CORRECT ANSWER IN THE SPACE AT THE RIGHT.*

1. If the seller in whom legal title is vested should die, the dower or curtesy right of the surviving spouse would vest, and, from that time up to the death of that surviving spouse, he, or she, would be entitled to the possession of an undivided one-half interest in the property. 1.____

2. An individual, other than the person holding the legal title, who has a life estate in the property is NOT a necessary party to the contract of sale as one of the sellers. 2.____

3. If the seller is a minor, the contract MUST be executed by the duly appointed guardian. 3.____

4. A minor has the option of declaring a contract valid or void when he reaches the age of maturity. 4.____

5. If the estate is that of an intestate descendant, it MUST be executed by an administrator. 5.____

6. If a contract is executed by a seller as a fiduciary named under a will, a trust or agency agreement MUST be shown. 6.____

7. An insufficient description of the property may render the contract void under the Statute of Frauds. 7.____

8. A land contract refers to the special situation in which the seller agrees to sell for a price payable in installments over a specified period of time, and to execute a deed ONLY upon full performance by the buyer. 8.____

9. The use of the land contract is increased during periods of tight money. 9.____

10. The right to possession follows legal title. 10.____

11. In a suit to foreclose a contract of sale, the court makes an interlocutory decree which decrees the amount due on the contract, gives to the buyer a specified time to pay in full the amounts found to be due, and provides that, in the event of the failure of the defendant to pay said amounts, the defendant be foreclosed of all right in the property covered by the contract. 11.____

12. The buyer in a contract of sale has a right of redemption. 12.____

13. In the event of a default in the payments under a contract of sale, the seller has the immediate right to go into possession of the property. 13.____

14. In the event of a default in the payments under a contract of sale, the buyer automatically and by operation of law loses all of his right in the property. 14.____

15. The ONLY way to take from the buyer his rights in the property is to foreclose the contract of sale or to secure a release from the buyer of his interest. 15.____

16. If the seller in a contract of sale accepts any payment upon the contract of sale even one day later, or if the seller accepts any performance on the contract of sale after a default by the buyer in the failure to pay taxes, the seller is deemed to have received the strict performance of the contract. 16.____

17. Where a buyer in a contract of sale has a judgment of record against him, he can make an assignment of the contract of sale and a transfer of his interest in the real property covered by the contract of sale, WITHOUT having the judgment vested as a lien on the property. 17.____

18. In the event of a default in payments on a contract of sale, the seller is limited in his remedies by the forfeiture clause of the contract. 18.____

19. It is essential for the husband or wife of the owner of the buyer's interest to join in the execution of any assignment of the contract. 19.____

20. Equitable conversion is the change of property from real to personal or from personal to real. 20.____

21. Such equitable conversion when the result of the execution of a contract is entirely physical. 21.____

22. In an equitable conversion, the seller has the right to receive the money and he also is the owner of the real property as trustee for the benefit of the buyer. 22.____

23. If the seller dies leaving a will, his interest in the property would be distributed as personal property to his legatees and NOT to his devisees. 23.____

24. An agreement to employ a broker to sell real property can ONLY be consummated and evidenced by a series of writings or notes. 24.____

25. An earnest money receipt that is NOT written is merely voidable. 25.____

KEY (CORRECT ANSWERS)

1.	T	11.	T
2.	F	12.	F
3.	T	13.	F
4.	T	14.	F
5.	T	15.	T
6.	T	16.	T
7.	T	17.	T
8.	T	18.	T
9.	T	19.	T
10.	T	20.	T
21.	F		
22.	T		
23.	T		
24.	T		
25.	F		

TEST 3

DIRECTIONS: Each question consists of a statement. You are to indicate whether the statement is TRUE (T) or FALSE (F). *PRINT THE LETTER OF THE CORRECT ANSWER IN THE SPACE AT THE RIGHT.*

1. A real estate transaction USUALLY involves three contracts: a preliminary contract, called *offer to purchase*, or *earnest money*; a binder contract, which comes into existence when the seller accepts the buyer's offer; and a third, more formal and longer term contract, called a land contract.   1.____

2. ONLY after title is found marketable is the particular deal *closed* by having a seller and buyer sign the second more formal and longer term contract called land contract.   2.____

3. If parties to a sale of land skip the preliminary contract and just sign the land contract in order to bind the deal, the buyer will make payments over a long period of time and NOT have the title checked until the final payment is almost due.   3.____

4. USUALLY the preliminary contract outlines the basic terms of the deal which are then repeated in the land contract.   4.____

5. The practice is to record a preliminary contract.   5.____

6. The preliminary contract is recordable since it is USUALLY acknowledged before a notary public or under seal.   6.____

7. Land contracts are USUALLY executed with the necessary formalities and are usually recorded in the records of the deeds office of the county in which the land is located.   7.____

8. The buyer becomes the owner of the land in equity from the moment that the contract, whether preliminary or land contract, becomes binding.   8.____

9. If the seller refuses to give the buyer a deed upon the buyer's tender of payment pursuant to a preliminary contract, the buyer can sue for specific performance.   9.____

10. After either contract is signed and before performance, if the buyer dies, the contract is treated as personal property in his estate.   10.____

11. A privilege given by the owner of real estate to another to buy the property at a specified price within a specified period of time is called an option.   11.____

12. In an option situation, both parties are bound equally.   12.____

13. If the period of the option expires before the optionee has accepted the offer, the option is dead and the owner may keep whatever the optionee has paid him for the now expired offer.   13.____

14. Under both the land contract and the option to buy, the purchaser commits himself to pay the money and take the land.   14.____

15. A determination that an offer signed by a prospect is really nothing but an offer for an option, may defeat a real estate broker's claim for his commission under a listing contract calling for a *sale* of the land.   15.____

16. Both a mortgage and a land contract may be used to secure a running line of credit, advances under which will be made from time to time for business or construction purposes. 16.____

17. With a land contract, the seller can sue the buyer for the money owing and get a money judgment. 17.____

18. The seller CANNOT, on the basis of a default on one installment, declare the whole amount due and sue for it. 18.____

19. The principal reason why a seller would choose a land contract rather than a mortgage is that, on default, a seller can sue for strict foreclosure on a land contract. 19.____

20. A seller who uses the strict foreclosure method to remedy a breach, can get a deficiency judgment for the unpaid balance. 20.____

21. The remedy of unlawful detainer by which landlords can oust tenants who do NOT pay their rent is available against buyers who default either on land contract payments or on mortgage payments. 21.____

22. There is a tax advantage to the seller if he sells on land contract rather than mortgage. 22.____

23. The seller can get the advantage of installment reporting of the capital gain from the sale by simply making sure that NO more than 30% of the purchase price is to be paid in the tax year in which the sale is consummated. 23.____

24. If a land contract contains a non-assignment clause forbidding assignment by the buyer WITHOUT the seller's consent, written consent by the seller will be needed for a mortgage transaction by the buyer. 24.____

25. Non-assignment clauses are often used in mortgages. 25.____

KEY (CORRECT ANSWERS)

1.	F	11.	T
2.	T	12.	F
3.	T	13.	T
4.	T	14.	F
5.	F	15.	T
6.	F	16.	F
7.	T	17.	T
8.	T	18.	F
9.	T	19.	T
10.	F	20.	F

21. F
22. F
23. T
24. T
25. F

EXAMINATION SECTION
TEST 1

DIRECTIONS: Each question consists of a statement. You are to indicate whether the statement is TRUE (T) or FALSE (F). *PRINT THE LETTER OF THE CORRECT ANSWER IN THE SPACE AT THE RIGHT.*

1. A prudent buyer of real estate will demand that the seller furnish proof or evidence of his (the seller's) ownership. 1.____

2. The fact that a seller can produce a deed to the property he is selling naming himself as grantee is adequate proof of ownership in the seller. 2.____

3. The prudent buyer should know the exact state of his seller's title. 3.____

4. The buyer's lender will NOT be greatly concerned with the state of the title since he accepted a mortgage on this property as security only for the repayment of the loan he made. 4.____

5. The ONLY true evidence of title is the county records. 5.____

6. The county records are EXTREMELY difficult and time consuming to examine so that the major evidence of title has become the abstract. 6.____

7. Any average purchaser can understand the state of the title by examining an abstract. 7.____

8. All states provide for the recording, in a public office, of EVERY document by which any estate or interest in land is created, transferred, encumbered or otherwise affected. 8.____

9. All documents affecting real property appear in the county clerk's records. 9.____

10. No documents affecting the rights in real estate shall be valid against any persons who do NOT have actual knowledge of the rights of the parties unless the document is recorded. 10.____

11. A donee of a parcel of land is protected against a previous buyer of the same piece of property who neglected to record his deed. 11.____

12. In a race-notice jurisdiction, the purchaser for value MUST win the race to the recording office and be without notice of the prior claim at the time he gave value. 12.____

13. The abstract of title is a summary of each and every recorded instrument affecting the title to the tract of real estate covered by the abstract and is compiled by a duly licensed abstracter. 13.____

14. An abstract of title MAY also include such filed instruments as security agreements, financing statements, chattel mortgages, and certain liens. 14.____

15. There in ONLY one type of title opinion. 15.____

16. The purchaser's title opinion is the chief instrument upon which the buyer relies. 16.____

17. It is wise for a buyer to rely on a mortgagee's opinion. 17.____

18. The abstracter is a guarantor of the title to the real estate. 18._____

19. If the abstracter negligently omits a document from the abstract or incorrectly summarizes the content of such instrument, he CAN be held liable for any loss caused the purchaser. 19._____

20. An attorney CAN be held liable for any loss caused by his failure to discover an existing, recorded lien contained in the abstract. 20._____

21. An abstract MAY indicate that the seller has clear title, but the chain of title may contain a forged deed. 21._____

22. There is no way of knowing from the abstract whether a deed is forged or not and, of course, such a deed passes no title. 22._____

23. An abstract will reveal the rights of parties in possession. 23._____

24. Title insurance is a contract which protects the insured against loss occurring through defects in title to real property. 24._____

25. A title insurance policy provides that the company will indemnify the owner against any loss that he may sustain because of a defect in the title to the real estate provided that the defect is specifically excluded in the policy. 25._____

KEY (CORRECT ANSWERS)

1.	T		11.	F
2.	F		12.	T
3.	T		13.	T
4.	F		14.	T
5.	T		15.	F
6.	T		16.	T
7.	F		17.	F
8.	T		18.	F
9.	F		19.	T
10.	T		20.	T

21. T
22. T
23. F
24. T
25. F

TEST 2

DIRECTIONS: Each question consists of a statement. You are to indicate whether the statement is TRUE (T) or FALSE (F). *PRINT THE LETTER OF THE CORRECT ANSWER IN THE SPACE AT THE RIGHT.*

1. The insurance company MUST be paid by the insured to defend any lawsuit attacking the title where such attack is based on a claimed defect which is covered by the insurance provisions. 1.____

2. Title insurance USUALLY insures against rights or claims of parties in possession not shown of record, including unrecorded easements. 2.____

3. Title insurance usually does NOT insure against any state of facts an accurate survey would show. 3.____

4. A mechanic's lien, or any rights thereto, where no notice of such lien or right appears of record, would USUALLY be insured by a policy of title insurance. 4.____

5. Taxes and assessments not yet due or payable and special assessments not yet certified to the treasurer's office, are NOT covered by title insurance. 5.____

6. The title insurance company guarantees against loss occuring because of defects existing at or before the date of the policy. 6.____

7. Defects which come into existence subsequent to the date of insurance of the title policy are USUALLY covered. 7.____

8. The fee or premium for a title insurance policy is much the same as with other insurance policies -- the fee is paid on a continuing annual basis. 8.____

9. The owner's policy is not transferable; therefore, when the property is resold, the new purchaser SHOULD obtain a reissue title policy. 9.____

10. The mortgagee's policy is normally transferable, so that if the note and mortgage are sold, the new mortgage need NOT obtain a reissue policy. 10.____

11. A mortgagee's policy protects the owner's interest in the property. 11.____

12. In the case of a mortgagee's policy, if the insurer pays the mortgagee, the insurance company could enforce the mortgage against the mortgagor. 12.____

13. Voluntary alienation or transfer of land by deed is by far the MOST commonly encountered method of transfer of title. 13.____

14. A deed is a written instrument dated and signed by the grantor which creates or conveys an interest in real estate to a named grantee. 14.____

15. A general warranty deed is one in which the grantor warrants or guarantees the title against defects existing before the grantor acquired title or arising during the grantor's ownership. 15.____

16. A general warranty deed warrants against encumbrances or defects arising from the grantee's own acts. 16.____

17. The covenants and warranties of a general warranty deed are obligatory and binding upon the grantor, his heirs and personal representatives.   17.____

18. If a grantor wishes to convey less than his entire interest in the property, he MUST spell out what is reserved or excepted in the general warranty deed.   18.____

19. A special warranty deed is one in which the grantor warrants or guarantees ONLY against claims asserted by, through, or under him.   19.____

20. A special warranty deed is one in which the grantor warrants the title against defects arising after he acquired the property and NOT against defects arising before that time.   20.____

21. The special warranty deed is MOST often used by persons holding title for someone else, such as a trustee or guardian.   21.____

22. A quitclaim deed is one in which the grantor warrants nothing.   22.____

23. A quitclaim deed is RARELY used to clear up a technical defect in the chain of title or to release lien claims against the property.   23.____

24. A deed MUST be recorded in order to be valied.   24.____

25. To be effective, a deed MUST be in writing.   25.____

KEY (CORRECT ANSWERS)

1.	F		11.	F
2.	F		12.	T
3.	T		13.	T
4.	F		14.	T
5.	T		15.	T
6.	T		16.	F
7.	F		17.	T
8.	F		18.	T
9.	T		19.	T
10.	T		20.	T

21. T
22. T
23. F
24. F
25. T

TEST 3

DIRECTIONS: Each question consists of a statement. You are to indicate whether the statement is TRUE (T) or FALSE (F). *PRINT THE LETTER OF THE CORRECT ANSWER IN THE SPACE AT THE RIGHT.*

1. A lease for a term of less than one year does NOT have to be in writing.   1.____

2. A date is ABSOLUTELY essential to a deed.   2.____

3. To be valid, a deed MUST designate the name of the grantor and the name MUST be identical to that appearing in the conveyance by which he received his title.   3.____

4. The grantor, if a natural person, SHOULD be of legal age and sound mind at the time of conveyance; otherwise the grantor can, at a later date, have the deed set aside and recover the property.   4.____

5. The grantee does NOT have to be named in the deed.   5.____

6. A deed WITHOUT legal consideration is not valid.   6.____

7. Generally, a donee CANNOT enforce covenants of warranty against the donor since said covenants are not supported by consideration.   7.____

8. A gift deed given to defraud creditors may NOT be set aside by the grantor's creditors.   8.____

9. A deed WITHOUT words of conveyance is ineffective.   9.____

10. The only words of conveyance are "sell and convey."   10.____

11. A deed is NOT valid unless it describes the real estate conveyed.   11.____

12. In transferring a house and lot it is necessary only to describe the land upon which the house is situated.   12.____

13. A grantor may NOT place restrictions upon the right to use the real estate conveyed.   13.____

14. Warranties and covenants are an essential requirement of a valid deed.   14.____

15. A deed is invalid UNLESS it is signed by the grantor.   15.____

16. If the property to be conveyed is homestead property, the owner's spouse MUST join in the conveyance.   16.____

17. A deed is NOT effective unless it is delivered by the grantor and accepted by the grantee.   17.____

18. If the deed is given to the grantee to afford him an opportunity to examine it, this constitutes a delivery.   18.____

19. For delivery of a deed to be effective, it MUST be made during the lifetime of the grantor.   19.____

20. An acknowledgment is a declaration made by a person to a notary public, or other public official authorized to take acknowledgments, that the instrument was executed by him and that it is his free and voluntary act.   20.____

21. Voluntary transfer of title during the lifetime of the owner is SELDOM accomplished by a written document known as a "deed." 21.____

22. So-called "statutory deeds" have been practically displaced by common law conveyances in MOST of the States. 22.____

23. The quitclaim deed can be safely used for passing title. 23.____

24. The bargain and sale deed is the highest form in order of obligation by the grantor and protection to the grantee. 24.____

25. Basically, the warranty deed is a bargain and sale deed with covenants. 25.____

KEY (CORRECT ANSWERS)

1. T
2. F
3. T
4. T
5. F

6. T
7. T
8. F
9. T
10. F

11. T
12. T
13. F
14. F
15. T

16. T
17. T
18. F
19. T
20. T

21. F
22. F
23. F
24. F
25. T

EXAMINATION SECTION
TEST 1

DIRECTIONS: Each question consists of a statement You are to indicate whether the statement is TRUE (T) or FALSE (F). *PRINT THE LETTER OF THE CORRECT ANSWER IN THE SPACE AT THE RIGHT.*

1. In 1916, New York City adopted the first comprehensive zoning ordinance in this country. 1.____

2. Since that time, American cities, with numerous exceptions, have adopted zoning ordinances so that now over 1,100 cities with populations in excess of 10,000 are zoned. 2.____

3. It is purely academic for the broker or salesman to be knowledgeable of planning, zoning, restrictive covenants, and other land use controls. 3.____

4. The purchaser, when he signs the usual form of purchase contract, agrees to take the land subject to restrictions of record, zoning, and other ordinances. 4.____

5. To the purchaser, use limitations are NOT usually so important as technical flaws on title that may be uncovered by examination of the abstract of title. 5.____

6. False information, intentionally or negligently given about land use restrictions, may be grounds for setting the sale aside. 6.____

7. Covenants that *run with the land* may be binding on those who inherit, buy or otherwise acquire the land after the owner of the land. 7.____

8. Restrictions imposed by subdivision developers are few in number and uniform in purpose. 8.____

9. Great care should be taken NOT to burden the land unduly because once on the land, they are hard to eliminate. 9.____

10. Many people, when the phrase *restrictive covenant* is used, think ONLY of racial or religious restrictions on land use. 10.____

11. Easements are SELDOM used by developers to implement their private plans. 11.____

12. *Conservation easements,* like privately imposed easements, will become increasingly important encumbrances on more and more tracts of land. 12.____

13. An existing filling station in a district zoned residential is an example of a non-conforming use. 13.____

14. For practical political reasons and in order to protect the zoning from attack on constitutional grounds, zoning ordinances uniformly permit the continuance of non-conforming uses. 14.____

15. An illegal use is one established before enactment of a zoning ordinance and in violation of it. 15.____

16. A method of bringing zoning into line with the prospective buyer's wishes is through the so-called zoning *variance.* 16.____

17. The zoning exception or special use permit is a method to meet the objectives of a prospective seller in appropriate cases. 17._____

18. It is a fact that the subdivider lays down an indelible land use pattern which will enhance or blight the community for generations to come. 18._____

19. The object of the official map is to preserve the land needed for future streets or for street-widening at bare land prices. 19._____

20. The restrictive covenant is the PRINCIPAL legal tool for the accomplishment of private land use planning goals. 20._____

21. Because land is rural, it is NOT zoned. 21._____

22. Zoning deals PRINCIPALLY with so-called bulk and density controls. 22._____

23. Land use planning may be both private and public. 23._____

24. In the absence of legal restraints, landowners exercising their broad common-law privileges of use may so use their land as to defeat both private or public planners goals and expectations. 24._____

25. Where a landowner stopped a non-conforming use some time ago and is now offering his premises for sale, the right to resume the use may have been lost by abandonment. 25._____

KEY (CORRECT ANSWERS)

1.	T	11.	F
2.	F	12.	T
3.	F	13.	T
4.	T	14.	T
5.	F	15.	F
6.	T	16.	T
7.	T	17.	F
8.	F	18.	T
9.	T	19.	T
10.	T	20.	T

21. F
22. F
23. T
24. T
25. T

TEST 2

DIRECTIONS: Each question consists of a statement. You are to indicate whether the statement is TRUE (T) or FALSE (F). *PRINT THE LETTER OF THE CORRECT ANSWER IN THE SPACE AT THE RIGHT.*

1. The real estate business in the United States is largely concerned with the land and buildings in highly concentrated areas of population which we call cities, metropolitan areas, or urban communities. 1.____

2. Zoning may retard value decline but it CANNOT prevent it. 2.____

3. There is little consistency in zoning symbols and descriptions in the political subdivisions of state government. 3.____

4. Government is involved in the real estate business at the federal level but NOT at the state and local levels. 4.____

5. The subdivision laws are designed primarily to protect the seller from misrepresentation, deceit, and fraud in the sale of new subdivisions by disclosing to the prospective purchaser the pertinent facts concerning the project. 5.____

6. Where one lot in a subdivision is made security for the payment of a trust, deed, note, or other lien or encumbrance to be satisfied with the payment of money, this is called a *blanket encumbrance*. 6.____

7. The power of eminent domain is the same as the *police power*. 7.____

8. The MAIN issue in almost all condemnation or eminent domain cases is the amount of *just compensation* required to be paid to the attorneys. 8.____

9. A defined channel is any natural watercourse even though dry during a good portion of the year. 9.____

10. If water is flowing in a defined channel, a landowner may obstruct or direct such water. 10.____

11. Waters overflowing a defined channel are considered *floodwaters,* and any landowner may protect himself from them by reasonable methods even though this might result in the floodwaters entering another man's land. 11.____

12. A purchaser of a condominium owns the air space in which his particular unit is situated in fee simple, has a deed thereto, gets a separate tax assessment, and may apply for and acquire a title insurance policy on his property. 12.____

13. Land development generally means the creation of a *subdivision.* 13.____

14. Before starting a land development program, the prudent developer will first contact the county surveyor. 14.____

15. *Subdivision* does NOT include certain types of multi-family structures. 15.____

16. A person may sell or offer for sale a lot or parcel of land in a subdivision pending final approval from the proper authorities. 16.____

17. The approval of the tentative map of the subdivision submitted to the planning commission constitutes a final approval of the plat for recording. 17._____

18. The survey and plat of the subdivision may be made by a surveyor who is NOT a registered engineer or a licensed land surveyor. 18._____

19. The plat of the subdivision must be of such a scale that survey and mathematical information and other details can be easily obtained from it. 19._____

20. Before a plat is approved, all taxes and assessments MUST be paid. 20._____

21. Before any sales can be made of subdivided lands, certain documents and instruments must be placed in escrow with a legal escrow depository. 21._____

22. The law prohibits any person selling or offering to sell lots or parcels in a subdivision from issuing, circulating, or publishing any prospectus. 22._____

23. The law prohibits any person selling or offering to sell lots or parcels in a subdivision from making any statement or representation UNLESS he declares that the real estate subdivision has been approved or indorsed by the commission. 23._____

24. The law prohibits any person selling or offering to sell lots or parcels in a subdivision from issuing, circulating, or publishing any advertising matter UNLESS he does so anonymously. 24._____

25. The real estate commission or commissioner is generally given authority to issue a *cease or desist* order whenever he finds a subdivider violating any provisions of the subdivision act. 25._____

KEY (CORRECT ANSWERS)

1. T
2. T
3. T
4. F
5. F

6. F
7. F
8. F
9. T
10. F

11. T
12. T
13. T
14. T
15. F

16. F
17. F
18. F
19. T
20. T

21. T
22. F
23. F
24. F
25. T

TEST 3

DIRECTIONS: Each question consists of a statement. You are to indicate whether the statement is TRUE (T) or FALSE (F). *PRINT THE LETTER OF THE CORRECT ANSWER IN THE SPACE AT THE RIGHT.*

1. The purchaser, when he signs the USUAL form of purchase contract, agrees to take the land exempt from restrictions of record, zoning, and other municipal ordinances. 1.____

2. False information, intentionally or negligently given about land use restrictions, MAY be grounds for setting the sale aside. 2.____

3. Standing silently by when you know the prospect is intending to use the land for a purpose forbidden by public or private restrictions will NOT endanger the sale unless the prospect is intentionally led astray. 3.____

4. It is important for the broker or salesman to know the ways in which zoning restrictions can be changed and whether or not a change in the zoning restrictions on a certain piece of property is possible to enhance the possibilities of a sale. 4.____

5. In the absence of legal restraints, land owners exercising their broad common law privileges of use may so use their land as to defeat both private or public planners' goals and expectations. 5.____

6. The easement is the PRINCIPAL legal tool for the accomplishment of private land use planning goals. 6.____

7. It is possible through covenants to set up virtually a private municipal government by creating a neighborhood association, giving it power to police the residential and other use restrictions, maintain streets, provide water, or render other services and assess charges against the benefited lots so as to raise the money needed to finance the services. 7.____

8. A covenant restriction is USUALLY of a very minor nature. 8.____

9. Covenants may NOT be recorded. 9.____

10. Once a covenant is in effect, it is binding and can NEVER be removed. 10.____

11. No state may act through its courts or otherwise to enforce racial or religious land use restrictive covenants. 11.____

12. Set-back, side yard, and back yard requirements are common restrictions imposed by covenants. 12.____

13. Presence of a covenant based on religion or race will bar Federal Housing Administration mortgage insurance and Veterans Administration financing. 13.____

14. Sometimes set-backs from the street take the form of easements established by declaration or grant. 14.____

15. Brokers and salesmen have an obligation to know about the existence of both publicly purchased and privately imposed easements as well as about restrictive covenants so that prospective buyers can be informed. 15.____

16. Zoning consists of dividing the land within a given governmental unit into districts and then specifying what uses are permitted and which ones prohibited in each district. 16.____

17. Zoning does NOT deal with the placement and height of buildings on the land and with bulk and density controls. 17.____

18. There are ONLY three types of zones: residential, commercial, and industrial. 18.____

19. In modern zoning plans, industry is barred from residential areas, but residences may be built in industrial areas. 19.____

20. It is safe to assume that rural land is unzoned. 20.____

21. A non-conforming use is one which was in existence when zoning went into effect and which is inconsistent with zoning purposes. 21.____

22. Zoning ordinances uniformly PROHIBIT the continuance of non-conforming uses in zoning ordinances. 22.____

23. There is USUALLY a prohibition against the expansion of non-conforming uses in zoning ordinances. 23.____

24. Once a non-conforming use has been abandoned, it can ALWAYS be re-established. 24.____

25. A landowner whose use is non-conforming may NOT sell his land and pass on the right to continue the use to the buyer. 25.____

KEY (CORRECT ANSWERS)

1. F
2. T
3. F
4. T
5. T

6. F
7. T
8. F
9. F
10. F

11. T
12. T
13. T
14. T
15. T

16. T
17. F
18. F
19. F
20. F

21. T
22. F
23. T
24. T
25. F

TEST 4

DIRECTIONS: Each question consists of a statement. You are to indicate whether the statement is TRUE (T) or FALSE (F). *PRINT THE LETTER OF THE CORRECT ANSWER IN THE SPACE AT THE RIGHT.*

1. Where a buyer is purchasing a non-conforming structure, the broker should warn him that in case of substantial destruction by fire or otherwise, zoning may bar rebuilding.   1.____

2. Where a landowner stopped the non-conforming use some time ago and now is offering his premises for sale, the right to resume the use may have been lost by abandonment.   2.____

3. There is no difference between a variance and a special use permit.   3.____

4. Wherever federal law is applicable, it is paramount.   4.____

5. Ordinarily, the basis of federal law is interstate commerce.   5.____

6. This is true of the U.S. Supreme Court case Jones v. Mayer and Title VIII of the Civil Rights Act of 1968.   6.____

7. Title VIII applies even to the MOST local transactions.   7.____

8. What discrimination state laws do NOT prohibit, federal law now does.   8.____

9. While no one may refuse to sell, lease, or rent to another because of race or color, a real estate licensee may do so when acting under his principal's directions.   9.____

10. Should a principal seek to restrict a listing according to race or color, the licensee MUST refuse to accept the listing.   10.____

11. Title VIII prohibits denial of membership or participation in a real estate board or multiple listing service to a person because of race, color, religion, or national origin, or discrimination against him in terms or conditions of membership.   11.____

12. Real estate licensees must not discriminate but they may accept restrictive listings.   12.____

Questions 13-22.

DIRECTIONS: In each of the following questions, a blank space indicates that a word or phrase has been omitted. Supply the missing word or phrase that will complete the statement correctly.

13. Before subdivided land can be sold or leased, a notice of _____ MUST be filed with the commissioner.   13.____

14. In MOST cases, the owner and subdivider are the same, but sometimes the owner will turn over the land to someone else to develop and assume necessary authority to offer it for sale. This person is commonly known as a _____.   14.____

15. The _____ type of subdivision is the kind MOST frequently developed.   15.____

16. A _____ is an estate in real property consisting of an undivided interest in common in a portion of a parcel of real property together with a separate interest in space in a residential, industrial, or commercial building on such real property, such as an apartment, office, or store, and may include, in addition, a separate interest in other portions of such property. 16.____

17. The power of eminent domain is _____ the *police power*. 17.____

18. The power of eminent domain involves a _____ and the payment of compensation to the property owner. 18.____

19. The use of the power of eminent domain is often referred to as _____. 19.____

20. The MAIN issue in almost all eminent domain cases is the amount of _____ required to be paid to the property owner. 20.____

21. _____ is a general principle underlying a vast body of detailed water law. 21.____

22. Waters overflowing a defined channel are considered _____. 22.____

Questions 23-25.

DIRECTIONS: In continuous discourse, briefly and concisely answer the following questions.

23. What is a stock cooperative? 23.____

24. What is meant by a blanket encumbrance. 24.____

25. What is meant by *fair market value*? 25.____

KEY (CORRECT ANSWERS)

1. T
2. T
3. F
4. T
5. T
6. F
7. T
8. T
9. F
10. T
11. T
12. F
13. intention
14. subdivider
15. standard
16. condominium

17. different from
18. taking
19. condemnation
20. just compensation
21. Conservation
22. floodwaters
23. A stock cooperative is a corporation which is formed or availed of primarily for the purpose of holding title to, either in fee simple or for a term of years, improved real property, if all or substantially all of the stockholders of such corporation receive a right of exclusive occupancy in a portion of the real property, title to which is held by the corporation, which right of occupancy is transferrable only concurrently with the transfer of the share or shares of stock in the corporation held by the person having such right of occupancy.
24. A blanket encumbrance is where more than one lot in a subdivision is made security for the payment of a trust deed note or other lien or encumbrance to be satisfied with the payment of money.
25. Fair market value is the highest price land would bring if exposed for sale in the open market with reasonable time allowed to find a purchaser with knowledge of all uses and purposes to which the land is adapted, the seller not being required to sell or the purchaser required to purchase.

EXAMINATION SECTION
TEST 1

DIRECTIONS: For each of the following questions, insert on the blank line the word or words which will CORRECTLY complete the statement or question. *PRINT THE CORRECT WORD OR WORDS IN THE SPACE AT THE RIGHT.*

1. A real estate broker's commission is deemed to have been earned by him at the _____.   1.____

2. An agreement of employment where the broker will collect a commission if anyone else, including the owner, sells the property, is called _____.   2.____

3. A person who employs an agent is called _____.   3.____

4. A document which transfers possession of real property, but does not convey ownership is _____.   4.____

5. When commercial property is being offered for sale, and a tenant wishes to renew a long-term lease, the managing broker should renew the lease with_____.   5.____

6. A transfer of part of a tenant's rights and interests under a lease to another is known as _____.   6.____

7. The lease of property in which the rental is based upon a percentage of the lessee's sales is called _____.   7.____

8. A written agreement which provides that an instrument or money be deposited with a third person to be delivered upon performance of a condition or conditions is called an _____.   8.____

9. An acquired legal privilege or right of use or enjoyment, falling short of ownership, which one may have in the land of another, is known as _____.   9.____

10. If your client insisted that title should close upon the exact date agreed upon, the provision which should be inserted in the contract to effect that end is called_____.   10.____

11. In order to protect his interests when an owner refuses to pay, a contractor should file a_____.   11.____

12. A contract is made for the sale of a parcel of real property. Before taking title to the property, and not being certain of the boundaries of the property, the purchase causes a_____ to be made.   12.____

13. A contract for the sale of an interest in real property is unenforceable unless such contract is in _____.   13.____

14. A wall built on the line separating two properties, partly on each, is called a _____.   14.____

15. A transfer or conveyance of the absolute ownership of property is a conveyance in _____.   15.____

16. The clause in a deed which indicates who is to convey the property and who is to receive the property is _____.   16.____

17. The covenant which guarantees absolute title to the premises forever is called the covenant of _____. 17._____

18. The ownership of realty by two or more persons, each of whom has an undivided interest, without the *right of survivorship,* is called_____. 18._____

19. A type of deed which is often used to remove a cloud from the title to real estate is the _____ deed. 19._____

20. The right of the people or government to take private property for public use is called _____. 20._____

21. The evidence of a personal debt which is secured by a lien on real estate, is called _____. 21._____

22. An instrument executed by the mortgagee setting forth the balance due on the mortgage as of the date of the execution of the instrument is called _____. 22._____

23. The clause which permits the placing of a mortgage at a later date which will take priority over an existing mortgage, is the _____. 23._____

24. The difference between the amount of mortgage indebtedness and the lesser amount realized at a foreclosure sale is called _____. 24._____

25. The higher price which a buyer, willing but not compelled to buy would pay, and the lowest price the seller, willing but not compelled to sell would accept, is called the _____. 25._____

3 (#1)

KEY (CORRECT ANSWERS)

1. time he brings about a meeting of the minds (or finds a buyer ready, willing, and able)
2. an exclusive right listing
3. a principal (or a client)
4. a lease
5. a cancellation clause
6. subletting
7. a percentage lease
8. an escrow agreement
9. an easement
10. *time is of the essence*
11. mechanic's lien
12. survey
13. writing
14. party wall
15. fee simple absolute
16. the granting clause
17. title guarantee
18. estate in common
19. quit claim
20. eminent domain
21. a bond
22. a mortgage reduction certificate
23. subordination clause
24. a deficiency
25. market value

TEST 2

DIRECTIONS: For each of the following questions, insert on the blank line the word or words which will CORRECTLY complete the statement or question. *PRINT THE CORRECT WORD OR WORDS IN THE SPACE AT THE RIGHT.*

1. A broker's powers or authority are limited to those _____. 1.____

2. A real estate salesman is considered to be,: an agent of _____. 2.____

3. An authorization is made in Texas for the sale of land located in New Mexico; such authorization is enforceable in accordance with the laws of _____. 3.____

4. Two competing brokers claim the commission on the negotiation of a real estate transaction, it is paid to the broker who_____. 4.____

5. The BEST way to determine the amount of compensation a broker will receive is the_____. 5.____

6. An outline of property prepared by a registered surveyor is known as a(n) _____. 6.____

7. If the contract of sale does not state a time for closing, then it is intended that the closing of the title be within a(n)_____. 7.____

8. A right to or interest in real estate that diminishes its value is called a(n) _____. 8.____

9. If the seller refuses to comply with the terms of his contract to sell real property and the buyer desires to possess the property, his legal remedy is to sue for _____. 9.____

10. Personal properties such as household goods or fixtures are called _____. 10.____

11. A legal right or claim upon a specific property which attaches to the property until a debt is satisfied, is called a(n)_____. 11.____

12. The right granted to the telephone company to erect telephone poles on another's property is called a(n) _____. 12.____

13. A contract by which the owner agrees with another person that he shall have a right to buy the property at fixed price within a certain time, is called a(n) _____. 13.____

14. A payment made to bind the bargain on the sale of real property is called _____. 14.____

15. A signed receipt reading as follows was given to a prospective purchaser of five lots in a subdivision: *Received from John Jones the sum of $50.00 on account of the purchase of five lots in Block X, balance $450.00; deed to be delivered on July 1, 2012.* 15.____

    John Jones has the right to refuse to complete his purchase because there is no proper _____ of the property sold.

16. An instrument that creates a lien on real estate as security for the repayment of a loan is called a(n) 16.____

17. The document which is filed to show that a mortgage is discharged of record is _____. 17.____

18. When a mortgage debt is past due, and the holder of the mortgage wishes to force the sale of the property to satisfy the debt, he starts an action in _____.   18.____

19. A mortgage which is taken back as part of the selling price is called _____.   19.____

20. An estate for years is referred to as a(n) _____.   20.____

21. In the assignment of a lease, a tenant-landlord relationship is created between the assignee and the _____.   21.____

22. A type of tenancy which may be terminated by either party at anytime is known as a tenancy _____.   22.____

23. A real estate broker drew a lease providing that the rent was to be paid MONTHLY, but did not specify therein that rent should be paid in advance. In such a case, the rent is due and payable on _____.   23.____

24. In order that it be recordable, a lease must be drawn for a period of more than three years *and* must be _____.   24.____

25. _____ in the amount for which property would sell if put upon the open market and sold in the ordinary manner.   25.____

KEY (CORRECT ANSWERS)

1. in the listing agreement
2. the broker
3. Texas
4. is the procuring cause
5. listing agreement
6. survey
7. reasonable period of time
8. encumbrance
9. specific performance
10. chattels
11. lien
12. easement
13. option
14. binder
15. description
16. mortgage
17. a satisfaction of mortgage
18. foreclosure
19. a purchase money mortgage
20. life estate
21. original tenant
22. at will
23. the end of the month
24. in writing
25. Market value

EXAMINATION SECTION
TEST 1

DIRECTIONS: Each question consists of a statement. You are to indicate whether the statement is TRUE (T) or FALSE (F). PRINT THE LETTER OF THE CORRECT ANSWER IN THE SPACE AT THE RIGHT.

1. A crime is NOT committed when the real estate licensing law is violated.   1._____

2. An auctioneer of real property is required to have a broker's license.   2._____

3. To become a licensed broker one must understand English.   3._____

4. An applicant for a license may be questioned as to his .trustworthiness.   4._____

5. The real estate licensing board may reject an application for a broker's license on the ground of untrustworthiness.   5._____

6. A broker need not post a sign in a branch office.   6._____

7. A broker may represent both the seller and buyer.   7._____

8. It is perfectly proper for a broker to insert blind ads in newspapers.   8._____

9. After a salesman's license has been revoked, he may never get it reissued.   9._____

10. If a broker's license is suspended, his salesmen's licenses are also suspended.   10._____

11. A prudent buyer of real estate will demand that the seller furnish proof of evidence of his (the seller's) ownership.   11._____

12. A licensed salesman may receive a commission from any person for whom he sells real estate.   12._____

13. When a broker discharges a salesman, he must make an affidavit for such discharge and send it to the real estate licensing board.   13._____

14. If a salesman's employment is terminated by mutual agreement, the broker must notify the real estate licensing board.   14._____

15. A broker is responsible for the civil wrongs of his salesmen.   15._____

16. To collect a commission by suit, the broker must allege that he is licensed.   16._____

17. To collect a commission, a broker must prove he is licensed.   17._____

18. There must be a complaint made before the real estate licensing board can take action.   18._____

19. A broker must keep a separate account for money belonging to a client.   19._____

20. A broker must account to his client for money collected by him.   20._____

21. As soon as a broker obtains a listing, he should place a sign on the building.   21._____

22. The BEST type of exclusive listing contract is one with an automatic renewal clause.   22._____

23. A broker should hire salesmen who can bring listings of former brokers with them.   23._____

24. A signed binder should immediately be delivered to the seller.   24._____

25. One mortgage covering several parcels of property is called a blanket mortgage.   25._____

KEY (CORRECT ANSWERS)

1. F	11. T
2. T	12. F
3. T	13. F
4. T	14. T
5. T	15. F
6. F	16. T
7. T	17. T
8. F	18. F
9. F	19. T
10. T	20. T

21. F
22. F
23. F
24. T
25. T

TEST 2

DIRECTIONS: Each question consists of a statement. You are to indicate whether the statement is TRUE (T) or FALSE (F). PRINT THE LETTER OF THE CORRECT ANSWER IN THE SPACE AT THE RIGHT.

1. A broker with the aid of a salesman sells a house; the owner refuses to pay a commission. The salesman cannot sue. 1.____

2. The mortgagor is the one who borrows the money. 2.____

3. The mortgagee is the one who takes back a mortgage. 3.____

4. The person assigning a mortgage is called assignee. 4.____

5. To create an effective lien, a mortgage must be recorded. 5.____

6. If the mortgagor refuses to pay the mortgage, the remedy of the mortgagee is foreclosure. 6.____

7. In a purchase money mortgage, the seller takes back a mortgage as part of the consideration. 7.____

8. At any time prior to the foreclosure sale, the mortgagor may pay off the mortgage plus the interest and the expenses. 8.____

9. An assignment of a mortgage is a conveyance. 9.____

10. A building and loan mortgage is a mortgage to secure funds while erecting a building. 10.____

11. A bank can lend money on a second mortgage. 11.____

12. A second mortgagee may be cut off in a foreclosure action. 12.____

13. As a general rule, the due date of a second mortgage should expire before the date of the first mortgage. 13.____

14. A real estate broker customarily acts as the agent for the buyer. 14.____

15. A general rule of the law of agency is that the act of the agent is the act of the principal. 15.____

16. A wife may act as the agent for her husband. 16.____

17. A broker may ratify an unauthorized act by his salesman. 17.____

18. By giving an exclusive right to sell his house, the owner may sell the house himself without liability. 18.____

19. If a broker has an exclusive agency, the owner may sell without any liability. 19.____

20. No agent may serve two principals without their consent. 20.____

2 (#2)

21. The authority of the agent to do a special act terminates when the act is done. 21.____

22. An agent's authority to sell real property must be in writing. 22.____

23. Every contract for the sale of real property must be in writing. 23.____

24. An offer cannot be accepted unless the acceptor knows of the offer. 24.____

25. A person may escape the terms of a contract because he signed it without reading. 25.____

KEY (CORRECT ANSWERS)

1. F	11. F
2. T	12. T
3. T	13. T
4. F	14. F
5. T	15. T
6. T	16. T
7. T	17. F
8. T	18. F
9. T	19. T
10. T	20. T

21. T
22. F
23. T
24. T
25. F

EXAMINATION SECTION
TEST 1

DIRECTIONS: Each question or incomplete statement is followed by several suggested answers or completions. Select the one that BEST answers the question or completes the statement. *PRINT THE LETTER OF THE CORRECT ANSWER IN THE SPACE AT THE RIGHT.*

1. A charge against a property owner to cover the proportionate cost of a street paving is a(n)

    A. ad valorem tax
    B. county tax
    C. assessment
    D. equitable obligation

    1.____

2. Whenever all parties agree to the terms of a real estate contract, there has been

    A. legality of object
    B. meeting of the minds
    C. reality of consent
    D. bilateral consideration

    2.____

3. At the time a buyer indicates he is ready to execute an agreement, the broker should obtain a

    A. trust deed
    B. negotiable note
    C. deposit
    D. surety

    3.____

4. Which of the following instruments is NOT delivered to the buyer at the closing of a sale?

    A. Deed
    B. Lease
    C. Affidavit of title
    D. Mortgage

    4.____

5. Under the usual form agreement of sale, the option to declare the deposit money forfeited belongs to the

    A. seller
    B. broker
    C. buyer
    D. real estate commission

    5.____

6. Anything that is fastened or attached to real property permanently is considered to be _____ property.

    A. personal   B. real   C. private   D. separate

    6.____

7. A payment made to bind a seller to the sale of real estate for a period of time is a(n)

    A. binder
    B. bond
    C. escrow agreement
    D. option

    7.____

8. In order to record a deed, it MUST be in writing and

    A. signed by the grantee
    B. recite the actual purchase price
    C. acknowledged
    D. be free from all liens

    8.____

9. Which of the following forms of deeds has one or more guarantees of title?

    A. Quit claim deed
    B. Warranty deed
    C. Executor's deed
    D. Bargain and sale

    9.____

129

10. Unpaid taxes on real estate become

    A. a lien
    B. an easement
    C. a judgment
    D. salable

11. The BEST way for the home owner to liquidate a mortgage debt is by

    A. the employer's withholding part of salary
    B. bank credit
    C. amortization
    D. having the savings bank account set off

12. The interest or value which an owner has in the property over and above the mortgage debt is known as a(n)

    A. escrow   B. equality   C. equity   D. surplus

13. A mortgage is released by

    A. revision
    B. reconveyance
    C. quit claim deed
    D. satisfaction

14. A mortgage which is partly due and subject to foreclosure at any time is called a(n) _____ mortgage.

    A. open   B. senior   C. primary   D. closed

15. A deed to be valid need NOT necessarily be

    A. signed   B. written   C. sealed   D. delivered

16. A document which transfers possession of real property but does NOT transfer ownership is a

    A. deed   B. mortgage   C. lease   D. deposition

17. The instrument which *conditionally* conveys title to real estate is a

    A. conditional bailment lease
    B. chattel mortgage
    C. mortgage
    D. land purchase contract

18. The party to whom a deed conveys real estate is called the

    A. grantee   B. grantor   C. beneficiary   D. recipient

19. The tax on a given piece of property is ALWAYS determined by multiplying the tax rate by the

    A. selling price
    B. assessed valuation of the property
    C. appraised valuation of the property
    D. market value

20. The description of land sold under an agreement of sale should 20.____

    A. give the house number and street
    B. give a full legal description
    C. describe the improvements
    D. state the metes and bounds

21. A salesman receiving a deposit should 21.____

    A. place it in his *special account*
    B. place it in the broker's general account
    C. turn it over to his broker
    D. deposit it in a bank

22. In listing property for sale, which item is NOT necessary for a valid exclusive listing agreement? 22.____

    A. Date of listing
    B. Address of property
    C. Legal description
    D. Listing period

23. BROKER is to SALESMAN as EMPLOYER is to 23.____

    A. principal   B. client   C. trainee   D. employee

24. A real estate listing is 24.____

    A. a list of all property held by one owner
    B. the employment of a broker by the owner to sell or lease real property
    C. a written list of improvements on the land
    D. the list of properties compiled by the local real estate board

25. An agent is one employed by the 25.____

    A. salesman   B. principal   C. master   D. broker

26. All real estate listed for sale by a broker should be advertised in the name of the 26.____

    A. seller
    B. salesman who obtains the listing
    C. salesman on the premises
    D. principal licensed broker

27. What is the MAXIMUM commission rate that a broker may charge on the sale of improved property? 27.____

    A. 6%
    B. 5%
    C. 10%
    D. Any rate agreed upon by the agent and principal

28. Blocks of real estate in a certain area are assessed at $200,000 each. The tax rate is 90¢ per $500. 28.____
    What amount of tax is due on each block?

    A. $540.00   B. $480.00   C. $360.00   D. $280.00

29. It is possible for an owner to have more than one agent in a certain situation, such as in the case of a(n) _____ listing.

    A. open
    B. multiple
    C. non-exclusive
    D. general

30. The FIRST step necessary for a licensed broker to recover a commission is to

    A. find a buyer
    B. find a seller
    C. have a contract of employment
    D. advertise the property for sale

31. In the real estate business, another term for principal is

    A. customer
    B. client
    C. head of company
    D. executive

32. A certain property is assessed at $550,000, and the tax rate is $4.85 per $1,000. What is the tax to be paid on this property?

    A. $2,567.50   B. $2,767.50   C. $2,867.50   D. $2,667.50

33. In the absence of a prior agreement, as to when the broker's commission is earned, such commission is earned at

    A. consummation of the deal
    B. a meeting of the minds of buyer and seller
    C. the time broker introduces buyer and seller
    D. when the deed is delivered

34. A contract which provides for the payment of a commission to a broker even though the owner makes a sale without the aid of the broker is called an

    A. exclusive listing agency
    B. open listing
    C. option
    D. exclusive right

35. When broker and salesman have a dispute over commission on a deal, they should

    A. complain to the owner
    B. bring action in court
    C. file a joint complaint to the state commission
    D. compel arbitration

36. To be enforceable, a listing must be signed by the

    A. broker
    B. seller
    C. owner
    D. real estate board

37. *Ethics* MOST NEARLY means

    A. observing usual closing hours
    B. belonging to the proper civic clubs
    C. observing duties to clients, colleagues, and public
    D. posting schedule of commissions and fees

38. An exclusive listing is a(n)

    A. listing given to several brokers
    B. implied listing
    C. net listing
    D. listing given to one broker only with an agreement not to list with other brokers during the term of the listing

38._____

39. A broker who sells a property to a purchaser recommended by a friend should

    A. thank the friend
    B. buy the friend a suitable gift
    C. give the friend all of the commission
    D. pay the friend 2% of the commission

39._____

40. An example of fiduciary relationship is that which exists between

    A. broker and prospect
    B. broker and anyone he talks to about real estate
    C. broker and client
    D. accountant and client

40._____

KEY (CORRECT ANSWERS)

1.	C	11.	C	21.	C	31.	B
2.	B	12.	C	22.	C	32.	D
3.	C	13.	D	23.	D	33.	B
4.	D	14.	A	24.	B	34.	D
5.	A	15.	C	25.	B	35.	B
6.	B	16.	C	26.	D	36.	B
7.	D	17.	D	27.	D	37.	C
8.	C	18.	A	28.	C	38.	D
9.	B	19.	B	29.	B	39.	A
10.	A	20.	B	30.	C	40.	C

EXAMINATION SECTION
TEST 1

DIRECTIONS: Each question consists of a statement. You are to indicate whether the statement is TRUE (T) or FALSE (F). *PRINT THE LETTER OF THE CORRECT ANSWER IN THE SPACE AT THE RIGHT.*

1. To have a valid contract there must be a *meeting of the minds.* 1.____
2. A contract for the sale of real property should contain a description of the property. 2.____
3. When a real property contract says: *Time is of the essence,* it means that the closing date may be adjourned by either party. 3.____
4. The real property contract should contain the price and terms of payments. 4.____
5. An offer may be terminated by death. 5.____
6. The instrument by which one may take possession of real property is a lien. 6.____
7. A lease must run for three years and be acknowledged to be recordable. 7.____
8. A lease is a contract. 8.____
9. Ordinary repairs are made by the tenant. 9.____
10. A lease for more than one year may be oral. 10.____
11. A tenant who retains possession beyond the term of his lease is known as a *statutory tenant.* 11.____
12. A lease may be voided if the premises are used illegally. 12.____
13. Security deposited under a lease may be used by the land-lord for repairs. 13.____
14. A landlord is the trustee for money deposited as security for a lease. 14.____
15. A lease is a contract; therefore, it is proper for the landlord and the tenant to allow the security to become an asset of the landlord. 15.____
16. The parties to a lease may agree to relieve the landlord of liability in case of negligence. 16.____
17. The tenant is automatically evicted in case his landlord's mortgage is foreclosed. 17.____
18. An action to evict a tenant is called a *summary proceeding.* 18.____
19. Under the rent laws, a landlord may demand additional rent for a television aerial. 19.____
20. A lease may be mortgaged. 20.____
21. Where the tenant leaves before the expiration of his lease, the landlord is entitled automatically to the balance or the rent as damages. 21.____
22. In an eviction for non-payment of rent, the money may be paid at any time before the final order is signed. 22.____

23. In general, a tenant must used the building for the purpose for which it was leased. 23._____

24. The lease cannot forbid assigning or subletting. 24._____

25. The tenant's basic right in a lease is the right of possession. 25._____

KEY (CORRECT ANSWERS)

1. T
2. T
3. F
4. T
5. T

6. F
7. T
8. T
9. T
10. F

11. F
12. T
13. F
14. T
15. T

16. F
17. F
18. T
19. T
20. T

21. F
22. T
23. T
24. F
25. T

TEST 2

DIRECTIONS: Each question consists of a statement. You are to indicate whether the statement is TRUE (T) or FALSE (F). *PRINT THE LETTER OF THE CORRECT ANSWER IN THE SPACE AT THE RIGHT.*

1. The lessor may reserve the right to use the roof for his own purposes. 1.____
2. In the absence of an agreement to the contrary, the rent is payable before the end of the period. 2.____
3. The lessor must pay the lessee interest on a deposit under a lease. 3.____
4. An option to purchase in a lease is enforceable in Surrogate's Court. 4.____
5. Income received from a lease is known as rent. 5.____
6. In the absence of a covenant to the contrary, a landlord may not come upon the tenant's property. 6.____
7. If a tenant damages the property, the landlord brings an action for waste. 7.____
8. If a man dies without heirs and without a will, his real estate escheats. 8.____
9. If a man dies without a will, he is said to have died intrastate. 9.____
10. If a man dies with a will, the man in charge of distributing the estate is called an administrator. 10.____
11. X is married and has one child and dies without a will. His wife gets one-third of his property. 11.____
12. A public utility may condemn property. 12.____
13. The city can pay whatever it likes in a condemnation proceeding. 13.____
14. In a condemnation proceeding the value of the property is frequently determined by a board of commissioners, who are often brokers. 14.____
15. An award in condemnation may not be appealed. 15.____
16. Land may be taken in condemnation for the private use of an individual. 16.____
17. More than one person can own real property at the same time. 17.____
18. An easement is an example of a non-possessory interest in real property. 18.____
19. An easement is a contract on which there is full agreement. 19.____
20. A right of way is a riparian right. 20.____
21. If A owns two lots and sells one to B, he may reserve an easement for himself in B's land. 21.____
22. If A uses B's land for a right of way for 15 years, he may get an easement by reservation. 22.____
23. A party wall may be an example of an easement. 23.____

24. An easement may be extinguished by release. 24.____

25. An easement may be extinguished by non-use. 25.____

KEY (CORRECT ANSWERS)

1. T
2. F
3. F
4. F
5. T

6. T
7. F
8. T
9. F
10. F

11. F
12. T
13. F
14. F
15. F

16. F
17. T
18. T
19. F
20. F

21. T
22. F
23. T
24. T
25. F

GLOSSARY OF REAL ESTATE TERMS

CONTENTS

	Page
Abstract of Title................Appraisal by Summation	1
Appurtenance........................Cancellation Clause	2
Caveat Emptor................................Conveyance	3
County Clerk's Certificate.... Documentary Evidence	4
Duress......................................Exclusive Agency	5
Exclusive Right to Sell.......................Ground Rent	6
Habendum Clause................................ Landlord	7
Lease..Mortgagee	8
Mortgagor...Party Wall	9
Percentage Lease....................................Release	10
Release Clause....................Subordination Clause	11
Subscribing Witness..............................Valuation	12
Vendee's Lien.... ....Zoning Ordinance	13

GLOSSARY OF REAL ESTATE TERMS

A

Abstract of Title—A summary of all of the recorded instruments and proceedings which affect the title to property, arranged in chronological order.

Accretion—The addition to land through processes of nature, as by streams or wind.

Accrued Interest—Accrue: to grow; to be added to. Accrued interest is interest that has been earned but not due and payable.

Acknowledgment—A formal declaration before a duly authorized officer by a person who has executed an instrument that such execution is the person's act and deed.

Acquisition—An act or process by which a person procures property.

Acre—A measure of land equaling 160 square rods or 4,840 square yards or 43,560 feet.

Adjacent—Lying near to but not necessarily in actual contact with.

Adjoining—Contiguous; attaching, in actual contact with.

Administrator—A person appointed by court to administer the estate of a deceased person who left no will; i.e., who died intestate.

Ad Valorem—According to valuation.

Adverse Possession—A means of acquiring title where an occupant has been in actual, open, notorious, exclusive, and continuous occupancy of property under a claim of right for the required statutory period.

Affidavit—A statement or declaration reduced to writing, and sworn to or affirmed before some officer who is authorized to administer an oath or affirmation.

Affirm—To confirm, to ratify, to verify.

Agency—That relationship between principal and agent which arises out of a contract either expressed or implied, written or oral, wherein an agent is employed by a person to do certain acts on the person's behalf in dealing with a third party.

Agent—One who undertakes to transact some business or to manage some affair for another by authority of the latter.

Agreement of Sale—A written agreement between seller and purchaser in which the purchaser agrees to buy certain real estate and the seller agrees to sell upon terms and conditions set forth therein.

Alienation—A transferring of property to another; the transfer of property and possession of lands, or other things, from one person to another

Amortization—A gradual paying off of a debt by periodical installments.

Apportionments—Adjustment of the income, expenses or carrying charges of real estate usually computed to the date of closing of title so that the seller pays all expenses to that date. The buyer assumes all expenses commencing the date the deed is conveyed to the buyer.

Appraisal—An estimate of a property's valuation by an appraiser who is usually presumed to be expert in this work.

Appraisal by Capitalization—An estimate of value by capitalization of productivity and income.

Appraisal by Comparison—Comparability with the sale prices of other similar properties.

Appraisal by Summation—Adding together all parts of a property separately appraised to form a whole: e.g., value of the land considered as vacant added to the cost of reproduction of the building, less depreciation.

Appurtenance—Something which is outside the property itself but belongs to the land and adds to its greater enjoyment such as a right of way or a barn or a dwelling.

Assessed Valuation—A valuation placed upon property by a public officer or a board, as a basis for taxation.

Assessment—A charge against real estate made by a unit of government to cover a proportionate cost of an improvement such as a street or sewer.

Assessor—An official who has the responsibility of determining assessed values.

Assignee—The person to whom an agreement or contract is assigned.

Assignment—The method or manner by which a right, a specialty, or contract is transferred from one person to another.

Assignor—A party who assigns or transfers an agreement or contract to another.

Assumption of Mortgage—The taking of title to property by a grantee, wherein the grantee assumes liability for payment of an existing note or bond secured by a mortgage against a property and becomes personally liable for the payment of such mortgage debt.

Attest—To witness to; to witness by observation and signature.

Avulsion—The removal of land from one owner to another, when a stream suddenly changes its channel.

B

Beneficiary—The person who receives or is to receive the benefits resulting from certain acts.

Bequeath—To give or hand down by will; to leave by will.

Bequest—That which is given by the terms of a will.

Bill of Sale—A written instrument given to pass title of personal property from vendor to vendee.

Binder—An agreement to cover the down payment for the purchase of real estate as evidence of good faith on the part of the purchaser.

Blanket Mortgage—A single mortgage which covers more than one piece of real estate.

Bona Fide—In good faith, without fraud.

Bond—The evidence of a personal debt which is secured by a mortgage or other lien on real estate.

Building Codes—Regulations established by local governments stating fully the structural requirements for building.

Building Line—A line fixed at a certain distance from the front and/or sides of a lot, beyond which no building can project.

Building Loan Agreement—An agreement whereby the lender advances money to an owner with provisional payments at certain stages of construction.

C

Cancellation Clause—A provision in a lease which confers upon one or more or all of the parties to the lease the right to terminate the party's or parties' obligations thereunder upon the occurrence of the condition or contingency set forth in the said clause.

Caveat Emptor—Let the buyer beware. The buyer must examine the goods or property and buy at the buyer's own risk.

Cease and Desist Order—An order executed by the Secretary of State directing broker recipients to cease and desist from all solicitation of homeowners whose names and addresses appear on the list(s) forwarded with such order. The order acknowledges petition filings by homeowners listed evidencing their premises are not for sale, thereby revoking the implied invitation to solicit. The issuance of a Cease and Desist Order does not prevent an owner from selling or listing his premises for sale. It prohibits soliciting by licensees served with such order and subjects violators to penalties of suspension or revocation of their licenses as provided in section 441-c of the Real Property Law.

Cease and Desist Petition—A statement filed by a homeowner showing address of premises owned which notifies the Department of State that such premises are not for sale and does not wish to be solicited. In so doing, petitioner revokes the implied invitation to be solicited, by any means with respect thereto, by licensed real estate brokers and salespersons.

Certiorari—A proceeding to review in a competent court the action of an inferior tribunal board or officer exercising judicial functions.

Chain of Title—A history of conveyances and encumbrances affecting a title from the time the original patent was granted, or as far back as records are available.

Chattel—Personal property, such as household goods or fixtures.

Chattel Mortgage—A mortgage on personal property.

Client—The one by whom a broker is employed and by whom the broker will be compensated on completion of the purpose of the agency.

Closing Date—The date upon which the buyer takes over the property; usually between 30 and 60 days after the signing of the contract. Cloud on the Title An outstanding claim or encumbrance which, if valid, would affect or impair the owner's title.

Collateral—Additional security pledged for the payment of an obligation.

Color of Title—That which appears to be good title, but which is not title in fact.

Commission—A sum due a real estate broker for services in that capacity.

Commitment—A pledge or a promise or affirmation agreement.

Condemnation—Taking private property for public use, with fair compensation to the owner; exercising the right of eminent domain.

Conditional Sales Contract—A contract for the sale of property stating that delivery is to be made to the buyer, title to remain vested in the seller until the conditions of the contract have been fulfilled.

Consideration—Anything of value given to induce entering into a contract; it may be money, personal services, or even love and affection.

Constructive Notice—Information or knowledge of a fact imputed by law to a person because the person could have discovered the fact by proper diligence and inquiry; (public records).

Contract—An agreement between competent parties to do or not to do certain things for a legal consideration, whereby each party acquires a right to what the other possesses.

Conversion—Change from one character or use to another.

Conveyance—The transfer of the title of land from one to another. The means or medium by which title of real estate is transferred.

County Clerk's Certificate—When an acknowledgment is taken by an officer not authorized in the state or county where the document is to be recorded, the instrument which must be attached to the acknowledgment is called a county clerk's certificate. It is given by the clerk of the county where the officer obtained his/her authority and certifies to the officer's signature and powers.

Covenants—Agreements written into deeds and other instruments promising performance or nonperformance of certain acts, or stipulating certain uses or nonuse's of the property.

D

Damages—The indemnity recoverable by a person who has sustained an injury, either to his/her person, property or relative rights, through the act or default of another.

Decedent—One who is dead.

Decree Order issued by one in authority; an edict or law; a judicial decision.

Dedication—A grant and appropriation of land by its owner for some public use, accepted for such use, by an authorized public official on behalf of the public.

Deed—An instrument in writing duly executed and delivered, that conveys title to real property.

Deed Restriction—An imposed restriction in a deed for the purpose of limiting the use of the land such as: A restriction against the sale of liquor thereon. A restriction As to the size, type, value or placement of improvements that may be erected thereon.

Default—Failure to fulfill a duty or promise, or to discharge an obligation; omission or failure to perform any acts.

Defendant—The party sued or called to answer in any suit, civil or criminal, at law or in equity.

Deficiency Judgment—A judgment given when the security for a loan does not entirely satisfy the debt upon its default.

Delivery—The transfer of the possession of a thing from one person to another.

Demising Clause—A clause found in a lease whereby the landlord (lessor) leases and the tenant (lessee) takes the property.

Depreciation—Loss of value in real property brought about by age, physical deterioration, or functional or economic obsolescence.

Descent—When an owner of real estate dies intestate, the owner's property descends, by operation of law, to the owner's distributees.

Devise—A gift of real estate by will or last testament.

Devisee—One who receives a bequest of real estate made by will.

Devisor—One who bequeaths real estate by will.

Directional Growth—The location or direction toward which the residential sections of a city are destined or determined to grow.

Dispossess Proceedings—Summary process by a landlord to oust a tenant and regain possession of the premises for nonpayment of rent or other breach of conditions of the lease or occupancy.

Distributee—Person receiving or entitled to receive land as representative of the former owner.

Documentary Evidence—Evidence in the form of written or printed papers.

Duress—Unlawful constraint exercised upon a person whereby the person is forced to do some act against his will.

Earnest Money—Down payment made by a purchaser of real estate as evidence of good faith.

Easement—A right that may be exercised by the public or individuals on, over or through the lands of others.

Ejectment—A form of action to regain possession of real property, with damages for the unlawful retention; used when there is no relationship of landlord and tenant.

Eminent Domain—A right of the government to acquire property for necessary public use by condemnation; the owner must be fairly compensated.

Encroachment—A building, part of a building, or obstruction which intrudes upon or invades a highway or sidewalk or trespasses upon the property of another.

Encumbrance—Any right to or interest in land that diminishes its value. (Also Incumbrance)

Endorsement—An act of signing one's name on the back of a check or note, with or without further qualifications.

Equity—The interest or value which the owner has in real estate over and above the liens against it.

Equity of Redemption—A right of the owner to reclaim property before it is sold through foreclosure proceedings, by the payment of the debt, interest and costs.

Erosion—The wearing away of land through processes of nature, as by streams and winds.

Escheat—The reversion to the state of property in event the owner thereof dies, without leaving a will and has no distributees to whom the property may pass by lawful descent.

Escrow—A written agreement between two or more parties providing that certain instruments or property be placed with a third party to be delivered to a designated person upon the fulfillment or performance of some act or condition.

Estate—The degree, quantity, nature and extent of interest which a person has in real property.

Estate for Life—An estate or interest held during the terms of some certain person's life.

Estate in Reversion—The residue of an estate left for the grantor, to commence in possession after the termination of some particular estate granted by the grantor.

Estate at Will—The occupation of lands and tenements by a tenant for an indefinite period, terminable by one or both parties at will.

Estoppel Certificate—An instrument executed by the mortgagor setting forth the present status and the balance due on the mortgage as of the date of the execution of the certificate. A legal proceeding by a lessor landlord to recover possession of real property.

Eviction, Actual—Where one is, either by force or by process of law, actually put out of possession.

Eviction, Constructive—Any disturbance of the tenant's possessions by the landlord whereby the premises are rendered unfit or unsuitable for the purpose for which they were leased.

Eviction, Partial—Where the possessor of the premises is deprived of a portion thereof.

Exclusive Agency—An agreement of employment of a broker to the exclusion of all other brokers; if sale is made by any other broker during term of employment, broker holding exclusive agency is entitled to commissions in addition to the commissions payable to the broker who effected the transaction.

Exclusive Right to Sell—An agreement of employment by a broker under which the exclusive right to sell for a specified period is granted to the broker; if a sale during the term of the agreement is made by the owner or by any other broker, the broker holding such exclusive right to sell is nevertheless entitled to compensation.

Executor—A male person or a corporate entity or any other type of organization named or designated in a will to carry out its provisions as to the disposition of the estate of a deceased person.

Executrix—A woman appointed to perform the duties similar to those of an executor.

Extension Agreement—An agreement which extends the life of the mortgage to a later date.

F

Fee; Fee Simple; Fee Absolute—Absolute ownership of real property; a person has this type of estate where the person is entitled to the entire property with unconditional power of disposition during the person's life and descending to the person's distributees and legal representatives upon the person's death intestate.

Fiduciary—A person who on behalf of or for the benefit of another transacts business or handles money on property not the person's own; such relationship implies great confidence and trust.

Fixtures—Personal property so attached to the land or improvements as to become part of the real property.

Foreclosure—A procedure whereby property pledged as security for a debt is sold to pay the debt in the event of default in payments or terms.

Forfeiture—Loss of money or anything of value, by way of penalty due to failure to perform.

Freehold—An interest in real estate, not less than an estate for life. (Use of this term discontinued Sept. 1, 1967.)

Front Foot—A standard measurement, one foot wide, of the width of land, applied at the frontage on its street line. Each front foot extends the depth of the lot.

G

Grace Period—Additional time allowed to perform an act or make a payment before a default occurs.

Graduated Leases—A lease which provides for a graduated change at stated intervals in the amount of the rent to be paid; used largely in long term leases.

Grant—A technical term used in deeds of conveyance of lands to indicate a transfer. Grantee The party to whom the title to real property is conveyed.

Grantor—The person who conveys real estate by deed; the seller.

Gross Income—Total income from property before any expenses are deducted.

Gross Lease—A lease of property whereby the lessor is to meet all property charges regularly incurred through ownership.

Ground Rent—Earnings of improved property credited to earning of the ground itself after allowance made for earnings of improvements.

H

Habendum Clause—The "To Have and To Hold" clause which defines or limits the quantity of the estate granted in the premises of the deed.

Hereditaments—The largest classification of property; including lands, tenements and incorporeal property, such as rights of way.

Holdover Tenant—A tenant who remains in possession of leased property after the expiration of the lease term.

Hypothecate—To give a thing as security without the necessity of giving up possession of it.

I

In Rem—A proceeding against the realty directly; as distinguished from a proceeding against a person. (Used in taking land for nonpayment of taxes, etc.)

Incompetent—A person who is unable to manage his/her own affairs by reason of insanity, inbecility or feeble-mindedness.

Incumbrance—Any right to or interest in land that diminishes its value. (Also Encumbrance)

Injunction—A writ or order issued under the seal of a court to restrain one or more parties to a suit or proceeding from doing an act which is deemed to be inequitable or unjust in regard to the rights of some other party or parties in the suit or proceeding.

Installments—Parts of the same debt, payable at successive periods as agreed; payments made to reduce a mortgage.

Instrument—A written legal document; created to effect the rights of the parties. Interest Rate—The percentage of a sum of money charged for its use.

Intestate—A person who dies having made no will, or leaves one which is defective in form, in which case the person's estate descends to the person's distributees.

Involuntary Lien—A lien imposed against property without consent of the owner, i.e., taxes, special assessments.

Irrevocable—Incapable of being recalled or revoked; unchangeable; unalterable.

J

Jeopardy—Peril, danger.

Joint Tenancy—Ownership of realty by two or more persons, each of whom has an undivided interest with the "right of survivorship."

Judgment—Decree of a court declaring that one individual is indebted to another, and fixing the amount of such indebtedness.

Junior Mortgage—A mortgage second in lien to a previous mortgage.

L

Laches—Delay or negligence in asserting one's legal rights.

Land, Tenements and Hereditaments—A phrase used in the early English Law, to express all sorts of property of the immovable class.

Landlord—One who rents property to another.

Lease—A contract whereby, for a consideration, usually termed rent, one who is entitled to the possession of real property transfers such rights to another for life, for a term of years, or at will. Leasehold The interest or estate which a lessee of real estate has therein by virtue of the lessee's lease.

Lessee—A person to whom property is rented under a lease.

Lessor—One who rents property to another under a lease.

Lien—A legal right or claim upon a specific property which attaches to the property until a debt is satisfied.

Lien (Mechanic's)—A notice filed with the County Clerk stating that payment has not been made for an improvement to real property. Life Estate The conveyance of title to property for the duration of the life of the grantee.

Life Tenant—The holder of a life estate.

Lis Pendens—A legal document, filed in the office of the county clerk giving notice that an action or proceeding is pending in the courts affecting the title to the property.

Listing—An employment contract between principal and agent, authorizing the agent to perform services for the principal involving the latter's property.

Litigation—The act of carrying on a lawsuit.

M

Mandatory—Requiring strict conformity or obedience.

Market Value—The highest price which a buyer, willing but not compelled to buy, would pay, and the lowest a seller, willing but not compelled to sell, would accept.

Marketable Title—A title which a court of equity considers to be so free from defect that it will enforce its acceptance by a purchaser.

Mechanic's Lien—A lien given by law upon a building or other improvement upon land, and upon the land itself, to secure the price of labor done upon, and materials furnished for, the improvement.

Meeting of the Minds—Whenever all parties to a contract agree to the exact terms thereof.

Metes and Bounds—A term used in describing the boundary lines of land, setting forth all the boundary lines together with their terminal points and angles.

Minor—A person under an age specified by law; under 18 years of age.

Monument—A fixed object and point established by surveyors to establish land locations.

Moratorium—An emergency act by a legislative body to suspend the legal enforcement of contractual obligations.

Mortgage—An instrument in writing, duly executed and delivered, that creates a lien upon real estate as security for the payment of a specified debt, which is usually in the form of a bond.

Mortgage Commitment—A formal indication, by a lending institution that it will grant a mortgage loan on property, in a certain specified amount and on certain specified terms. Mortgage Reduction Certificate An instrument executed by the mortgagee, setting forth the present status and the balance due on the mortgage as of the date of the execution of the instrument.

Mortgagee—The party who lends money and takes a mortgage to secure the payment thereof.

Mortgagor—A person who borrows money and gives a mortgage on the person's property as security for the payment of the debt.

Multiple Listing—An arrangement among Real Estate Board of Exchange Members, whereby each broker presents the broker's listings to the attention of the other members so that if a sale results, the commission is divided between the broker bringing the listing and the broker making the sale.

N

Net Listing—A price below which an owner will not sell the property, and at which price a broker will not receive a commission; the broker receives the excess over and above the net listing as the broker's commission.

Notary Public—A public officer who is authorized to take acknowledgments to certain classes of documents, such as deeds, contracts, mortgages, and before whom affidavits may be sworn.

O

Obligee—The person in whose favor an obligation is entered into.

Obligor—The person who binds himself/herself to another; one who has engaged to perform some obligation; one who makes a bond.

Obsolescence—Loss in value due to reduced desirability and usefulness of a structure because its design and construction become obsolete; loss because of becoming old-fashioned, and not in keeping with modern means, with consequent loss of income.

Open End Mortgage—A mortgage under which the mortgagor may secure additional funds from the mortgagee, usually up to but not exceeding the original amount of the existing amortizing mortgage.

Open Listing—A listing given to any number of brokers without liability to compensate any except the one who first secures a buyer ready, willing and able to meet the terms of the listing, or secures the acceptance by the seller of a satisfactory offer; the sale of the property automatically terminates the listing.

Open Mortgage—A mortgage that has matured or is overdue and, therefore, is "open" to foreclosure at any time.

Option—A right given for a consideration to purchase or lease a property upon specified terms within a specified time; if the right is not exercised the option holder is not subject to liability for damages; if exercised, the grantor of option must perform.

P

Partition—The division which is made of real property between those who own it in undivided shares.

Party Wall—A party wall is a wall built along the line separating two properties, partly on each, which wall either owner, the owner's heirs and assigns has the right to use; such right constituting an easement over so much of the adjoining owner's land as is covered by the wall.

Percentage Lease—A lease of property in which the rental is based upon the percentage of the volume of sales made upon the leased premises, usually provides for minimum rental.

Personal Property—Any property which is not real property.

Plat Book—A public record containing maps of land showing the division of such land into streets, blocks and lots and indicating the measurements of the individual parcels.

Plottage—Increment in unity value of a plot of land created by assembling smaller ownerships into one ownership.

Police Power—The right of any political body to enact laws and enforce them, for the order, safety, health, morals and general welfare of the public.

Power of Attorney—A written instrument duly signed and executed by an owner of property, which authorizes an agent to act on behalf of the owner to the extent indicated in the instrument.

Premises—Lands and tenements; an estate; the subject matter of a conveyance.

Prepayment Clause—A clause in a mortgage which gives a mortgagor the privilege of paying the mortgage indebtedness before it becomes due.

Principal—The employer of an agent or broker; the broker's or agent's client.

Probate—To establish the will of a deceased person.

Purchase Money Mortgage—A mortgage given by a grantee in part payment of the purchase price of real estate.

Q

Quiet Enjoyment—The right of an owner or a person legally in possession to the use of property without interference of possession.

Quiet Title Suit—A suit in court to remove a defect, cloud or suspicion regarding legal rights of an owner to a certain parcel of real property.

Quitclaim Deed—A deed which conveys simply the grantor's rights or interest in real estate, without any agreement or covenant as to the nature or extent of that interest, or any other covenants; usually used to remove a cloud from the title.

R

Real Estate Board—An organization whose members consist primarily of real estate brokers and salespersons.

Real Property—Land, and generally whatever is erected upon or affixed thereto.

Realtor—A coined word which may only be used by an active member of a local real estate board, affiliated with the National Association of Real Estate Boards.

Recording—The act of writing or entering in a book of public record instruments affecting the title to real property.

Redemption—The right of a mortgagor to redeem the property by paying a debt after the expiration date and before sale at foreclosure; the right of an owner to reclaim the owner's property after the sale for taxes.

Release—The act or writing by which some claim or interest is surrendered to another.

Release Clause—A clause found in a blanket mortgage which gives the owner of the property the privilege of paying off a portion of the mortgage indebtedness, and thus freeing a portion of the property from the mortgage.

Rem—(See In Rem)

Remainder—An estate which takes effect after the termination of a prior estate such as a life estate.

Remainderman—The person who is to receive the property after the death of a life tenant.

Rent—The compensation paid for the use of real estate.

Reproduction Cost—Normal cost of exact duplication of a property as of a certain date.

Restriction—A limitation placed upon the use of property contained in the deed or other written instrument in the chain of title. Reversionary Interest The interest which a person has in lands or other property upon the termination of the preceding estate.

Revocation—An act of recalling a power of authority conferred, as the revocation of a power of attorney, a license, an agency, etc.

Right of Survivorship—Right of the surviving joint owner to succeed to the interests of the deceased joint owner, distinguishing feature of a joint tenancy or tenancy by the entirety.

Right of Way—The right to pass over another's land more or less frequently according to the nature of the easement.

Riparian Owner—One who owns land bounding upon a river or watercourse.

Riparian Rights—The right of a landowner to water on, under or adjacent to his land.

S

Sales Contract—A contract by which the buyer and seller agree to terms of sale.

Satisfaction Piece—An instrument for recording and acknowledging payment of an indebtedness secured by a mortgage.

Seizin—The possession of land by one who claims to own at least an estate for life therein.

Set Back—The distance from the curb or other established line, within which no buildings may be erected.

Severalty—The ownership of real property by an individual, as an individual.

Special Assessment—An assessment made against a property to pay for a public improvement by which the assessed property is supposed to be especially benefited.

Specific Performance—A remedy in a court of equity compelling a defendant to carry out the terms of an agreement or contract.

Statute—A law established by an act of the Legislature.

Statute of Frauds—State law which provides that certain contracts must be in writing in order to be enforceable at law.

Stipulations—The terms within a written contract.

Straight Line Depreciation—A definite sum set aside annually from income to pay costs of replacing improvements, without reference to the interest it earns.

Subdivision—A tract of land divided into lots or plots suitable for home building purposes.

Subletting—A leasing by a tenant to another, who holds under the tenant.

Subordination Clause—A clause which permits the placing of a mortgage at a later date which takes priority over an existing mortgage.

Subscribing Witness—One who writes his/her name as witness to the execution of an instrument.

Surety—One who guarantees the performance of another; guarantor.

Surrender—The cancellation of a lease by mutual consent of the lessor and the lessee.

Surrogate's Court (Probate Court)—A court having jurisdiction over the proof of wills, the settling of estates and of citations.

Survey—The process by which a parcel of land is measured and its area ascertained; also the blueprint showing the measurements, boundaries and area.

T

Tax Sale—Sale of property after a period of nonpayment of taxes.

Tenancy in Common—An ownership of realty by two or more persons, each of whom has an undivided interest, without the "right of survivorship."

Tenancy by the Entirety—An estate which exists only between husband and wife with equal right of possession and enjoyment during their joint lives and with the "right of survivorship."

Tenancy at Will—A license to use or occupy lands and tenements at the will of the owner.

Tenant—One who is given possession of real estate for a fixed period or at will.

Tenant at Sufferance—One who comes into possession of lands by lawful title and keeps it afterwards without any title at all.

Testate—Where a person dies leaving a valid will.

Title—Evidence that owner of land is in lawful possession thereof; evidence of ownership.

Title Insurance—A policy of insurance which indemnifies the holder for any loss sustained by reason of defects in the title.

Title Search—An examination of the public records to determine the ownership and encumbrances affecting real property.

Torrens Title—System of title records provided by state law: it is a system for the registration of land titles whereby the state of the title, showing ownership and encumbrances, can be readily ascertained from an inspection of the "register of titles" without the necessity of a search of the public records.

Tort—A wrongful act, wrong, injury; violation of a legal right.

Transfer Tax—A tax charged under certain conditions on the property belonging to an estate.

U

Unearned Increment—An increase in value of real estate due to no effort on the part of the owner; often due to increase in population.

Urban Property—City property; closely settled property.

Usury—On a loan, claiming a rate of interest greater than that permitted by law.

V

Valid—Having force, or binding force; legally sufficient and authorized by law.

Valuation—Estimated worth or price. The act of valuing by appraisal.

Vendee's Lien—A lien against property under contract of sale to secure deposit paid by a purchaser.

Verification—Sworn statements before a duly qualified officer to the correctness of the contents of an instrument.

Violations—Act, deed or conditions contrary to law or permissible use of real property.

Void—To have no force or effect; that which is unenforceable.

Voidable—That which is capable of being adjudged void, but is not void unless action is taken to make it so.

W

Waiver—The renunciation, abandonment or surrender of some claim, right or privilege.

Warranty Deed—A conveyance of land in which the grantor warrants the title to the grantee.

Will—The disposition of one's property to take effect after death.

Without Recourse—Words used in endorsing a note or bill to denote that the future holder is not to look to the endorser in case of nonpayment.

Z

Zone—An area set off by the proper authorities for specific use; subject to certain restrictions or restraints.

Zoning Ordinance—Act of city or county or other authorities specifying type and use to which property may be put in specific areas.

www.ingramcontent.com/pod-product-compliance
Lightning Source LLC
Chambersburg PA
CBHW082046300426
44117CB00015B/2633